From Great Broughton to
Peter Gorley – Rugby Leag

CW00449285

By Peter Cropp__.

LONDON LEAGUE PUBLICATIONS LTD

From Great Broughton to Great Britain
Peter Gorley – Rugby League Forward

A CIP catalogue record for this book is available from the British Library.

First published in Great Britain in April 2004 by:
London League Publications Ltd, P.O. Box 10441, London E14 8WR

ISBN: 1-903659-16-7

Cover design by: Stephen McCarthy Graphic Design
                         46, Clarence Road, London N15 5BB

Layout: Peter Lush

Printed and bound by: Biddles Ltd
                         King's Lynn, Great Britain

Foreword: A tribute to Peter Gorley

It came as no surprise to find out a biography was being written about Peter, and it gives me great pleasure to say a few words.

Peter was an outstanding rugby league forward, and was the type of player you had to have on your team. A workhorse who gave 100 per cent every game, he was a smart player who had the ability to break the defence with a pass or by sheer strength and power.

He formed a formidable partnership with his brother Les, and it was a great pleasure to work with him as a player and coach.

Not many Cumbrians get the opportunity to play for St Helens, but Saints saw the potential in Peter and took the opportunity to sign him, Peter returned the favour by producing top class football for them.

Peter was a footballer who always gave his best in training and playing, that's the way he was, dedicated, a good listener and motivator who always produced the goods on the field.

Like many footballers he always enjoyed a pint of beer, it was his way of relaxing, but come the weekend, he was always looking forward to playing the game of rugby.

All the best Peter.

Paul Charlton

Paul Charlton is regarded as the best full-back from Cumberland. He joined Workington Town in 1960, and played 244 games, scoring 79 tries and 77 goals. He then was signed by Salford for a then world record transfer fee of £12,500. He played a further 234 games for Salford, scoring 99 tries. In 1975, he returned to Workington Town as player-coach, which included captaining them in four consecutive Lancashire Cup Finals. He finished his career with a brief spell at Blackpool Borough in 1981. In total, he played 727 first team games in a career of over 20 years. He won 19 test caps for Great Britain, one for England and played for Cumberland 32 times between 1965 and 1979.

Introduction

"Cumbrian Peter Gorley, who played for Saints in the 1980s, is seeking memorabilia of his days at Knowsley Road." An article in the St Helens local paper caught my attention. I had no memorabilia as such, apart from my programme collection, but I did have two things: memories of Peter's career and a desire to write. An opportunity had presented itself.

Peter Gorley was certainly a favourite of mine during his time at Saints. He was a top class forward who never gave less than 100 per cent effort, he missed very few games and was arguably the most reliable and consistent performer for the team which, until the later stages of his St Helens career, was in something of a transitional phase.

It also appealed to me that Peter had moved from Workington Town, the team I had always regarded as my second favourite. This probably stemmed from the time I was very young - considered too young to be taken to Knowsley Road, even - when my parents used to take me to visit Mum's old college friend in Brigham, a small village just outside Cockermouth. I became very fond of West Cumbria, as I still am today. Mum's friend's husband Walter Rees took an interest in sport in Workington, and would readily discuss rugby league with my Dad.

When I began to read about rugby league history I learned that Workington had been a power in the land and they had assumed this status very quickly after their formation at the end of the Second World War. It struck me as admirable that a team from a small town, remote from the game's heartlands, could be so successful. I admired their triumphs and was sad about their decline.

Helped by Peter and his team mates, the club was able to recapture the glory days through their Lancashire Cup exploits and Workington Town was back on the rugby league map. The players became household names. Inevitably some of the bigger clubs began to wonder whether their teams would benefit from the inclusion of Cumbrian talent. St Helens, among others, certainly did.

I wrote to Peter with my idea; he replied, and later we spoke on the telephone. We have met and chewed the fat in both Cumbria and Lancashire. He has provided much interesting information and material but always modestly. He clearly enjoyed his career but it is almost as if he doesn't regard it as a story worth relating. I beg to differ.

Peter Cropper
April 2004

About the author

Peter Cropper was born in St Helens six months after Saints' first Wembley triumph and has been a supporter since his Dad took him to what he considers to be the world's greatest rugby ground in 1965. He is married to Josephine and he lives in Horwich near Bolton, while daughter Hanne lives near Halifax. He is a writer, runs a home-based network marketing business and is a part time delivery driver. In his spare time, as well as rugby league, he watches football and cricket, and enjoys walking and playing in local quiz leagues.

Bibliography

Workington Town RLFC - A Fifty Year History by Joe Holliday
(Richard Matthew Publications 1996)
Cumberland Rugby League - 100 Greats by Robert Gate
(Tempus Publishing Ltd 2002)
The Memoirs and Sporting Life of Tom Mitchell - An Autobiography
(Echotime Inc. 1998)
Marching On - A Celebration of St Helens RLFC at the Millennium by Alex Service and Denis Whittle
(St Helens RLFC 1999)
The Shopacheck Rugby League Yearbook 1980-81 by David Howes and Raymond Fletcher (Educational Design Ltd 1980)
Rothmans Rugby League Yearbook 1981-82 to *1987-88* inclusive by Raymond Fletcher and David Howes (Rothmans Publications & Queen Anne Press)

Acknowledgements

I would like to thank everyone who has helped me in the production of this book. Peter and his friend Virginia have spent a lot of time with me reminiscing - sometimes over pints of Jennings, sometimes trying to exhaust Keswick's coffee supplies - and I am also grateful to Peter's former colleagues who have given their time to talk about him and who have contributed to the book.

I must also thank fellow rugby league writers, particularly Robert Gate, who provided the statistics, and Keith Nutter, who have given me great help and encouragement, and the two experts in matters of St Helens rugby league, Alex Service and Denis Whittle, who have kindly provided photographs and information. Thanks are also due to Ted Clifton of Ted's Gym in Workington who also loaned me his photographs of Peter, and the *Workington Times & Star* for providing photos.

The gaps in my programme collection were filled by fellow Saints traveller Ken Rigby and my Mum on the occasions I was missing from Knowsley Road, and the information contributed in that way has proved vital as was the technical expertise offered by family members Joe, Andrew and Jessica Mehers which helped with the scanning of the photographs. Thanks are also obviously due to Peter Lush and Dave Farrar at London League Publications who agreed to publish, thus helping me realise an ambition; to Michael O'Hare for sub-editing, Steve McCarthy for producing the cover and the staff at Biddles Ltd who printed the book.

I must also thank my wife Josephine and daughter Hanne for their support and encouragement at all times throughout the project. I dedicate the book to my Dad who sadly died in 1978. He saw Peter play for Workington but, sadly, not for Saints and he introduced me to the greatest of all games. Without his influence, there would be no book.

Peter Cropper

Contents

1. The early days

This is a story of a fine and underrated Rugby League player. He played for St Helens, one of the biggest names in the game, and is a member of its '200 club' having made 234 appearances between 1979 and 1986, scoring 46 tries in this time - a remarkable strike rate for a forward. And, amazingly, throughout his Saints career, he lived nowhere near the ground - training and home matches involved a round trip of more than 250 miles because he preferred to live in the county of his birth.

Prior to his transfer to St Helens he appeared with distinction on 124 occasions for Workington Town, his local professional team, scoring 13 tries. Altogether, he holds three winners medals (two Lancashire Cup, one Premiership), eight Cumbrian county caps, three England caps and three Great Britain caps. These statistics plus the loyalty and dedication which he displayed during his career make him, beyond any doubt, one of the top players of his generation. It is, without question, a story worth telling.

Peter Gorley was born on 10 July 1951 in Maryport on the West Cumbrian coast. Named after the wife of Colonel Humphrey Senhouse, the man who financed the building of the town's harbour, Maryport's importance lessened with the decline of the industries - notably coal mining - which it supported, and it had taken on rather a forlorn air. Now it is recovering and steps have been taken to regenerate it with tourist attractions such as the Roman Museum, Maritime Museum and aquarium which have made the town a good destination for those visitors to the Lake District who are willing to explore a little further afield.

Peter didn't grow up on the coast, but rather in the Cockermouth district a few miles inland. Cockermouth, where the River Cocker, having flowed through the picturesque Vale of Lorton, empties into the River Derwent, is a pleasant, unassuming market town about halfway between Keswick and the coast where the Rugby League strongholds of Workington and Whitehaven can be found. It is not really on the tourist trail, it is more of a working place of some character, but it also has much to offer discerning visitors such as those in search of the poet William Wordsworth's birthplace or an

1

informative tour of Jennings Brewery complete with a short stay in the sampling room. Many tourists miss Cockermouth and it is to their loss. The town and surrounding villages such as Brigham and Great Broughton - where Peter now lives - have an atmosphere of their own; they are unspoilt and undisturbed places which can be enjoyed quietly.

It was in this area where Peter grew up with his two brothers Les and Mitchell, both of whom, like Peter, were to enjoy rugby careers. Mitch, Peter's younger brother, played with Broughton Red Rose amateur rugby league team and Cockermouth rugby union club while Les, a year older than Peter, was to play more than 200 games of rugby league for Workington Town before joining a star-studded Widnes team at the height of its trophy winning powers. Les, too, was recognised as being one of the foremost forwards of his generation and, like Peter, represented his county and country with great distinction.

With the rest of the children in the village Peter attended Broughton Primary School before moving to Cockermouth Derwent School to continue his education at secondary level. He enjoyed maths, English, geography and history but at this stage he did not show a lot of interest in sport.

He played rugby union when the school team was short: "to make up the numbers," he said, probably modestly, but because he had no particular sporting inclination, he didn't much enjoy it. His interest in sport developed when he began to play rugby league with the other Broughton lads when he was a little older. They would take a ball down to the field and run around with much enthusiasm but, as lads of that age often do - Peter was about 15 - without much method, rhyme or reason. Someone was required to guide the young talent and to give it direction and discipline so that it could be moulded into a team.

The man for the job was Brian Campbell, a Baptist minister. He had no coaching qualifications but he had sufficient rugby league knowledge and bags of enthusiasm. Under Brian's guidance the lads became fitter and more aware of tactics. Progress was such that before very long they were able to enter a team into a league at under-19 level. Although Peter was about six feet tall he had yet to 'fill out' and he didn't play regularly in the earlier days. Later, of course, he was to become a key team member.

The team travelled to away fixtures in a converted dinner van, which had previously transported school meals around Cumbria, which Brian had bought and they would visit such famous rugby league locations as Egremont and Whitehaven. Although some hammerings had to be endured - 78-0 at Kells in Whitehaven sticks in Peter's mind - the team persevered and developed into the Broughton Red Rose team which still plays today.

The lads all respected Brian because he kept them occupied and taught them ideals and principles while giving up much of his own time to help them and provide them with new experiences. To take boys in the 14 to 16 age range camping and to see the sights of London took commitment - courage, even - and, of course, enthusiasm which Brian had in abundance. Broughton's sporting youth was eternally grateful to Brian Campbell and, although they never knew of him, the fans of Workington and St Helens should also be thankful. Later he was replaced as coach by John Whitehead. He was succeeded as coach by former Workington player Jackie Newell.

Red Rose

Peter played for Red Rose from its formation in 1967-68, moving through the under-17 team to the under-19s to open age level. His rugby skills developed, as did those of his team mates, and a strong camaraderie was built among the players. He also played for Maryport under-19s, and was in their side in a cup final against Egremont at Whitehaven.

He played with the Broughton team until he was 22 and he was proud to represent his county. He particularly recalls a county fixture against Lancashire at Salford in which he was named man-of-the-match and it seemed that selection for the Great Britain amateur team was inevitable. However, this was 1973, the year of the British Amateur Rugby League Association's formation, no national team was selected so Peter had to live with the disappointment.

Elder brother Les was now firmly establishing himself in Workington's pack having made his debut there in March 1971, and

Peter inevitably began to wonder whether he, too, would be able to play at professional level.

His big break arrived when he went to Workington with his dad to watch a Great Britain representative side. The occasion was a testimonial match for Howard 'Smiler' Allen, Town's stalwart hooker who played more than 200 games for the club as well as starring for Blackpool Borough in their moment of glory when they took Castleford the distance in the John Player Trophy final in 1977. Smiler also featured in a John Player Trophy final four years later playing with Barrow. He was one of those underrated, 100 per cent players who deserved to receive greater recognition for his efforts.

One of the Great Britain players was absent unexpectedly and Peter was asked by Ike Southward, one of the all time Cumbrian greats and a true legend in the game, if he could fill in. Despite a broken thumb which would have dissuaded a player of lesser courage, Peter agreed to play, ignoring his dad's protests. He simply could not resist the chance of playing with top-class players: "If you can't play with good players, then you probably didn't have the ability anyway to begin with," he says. Playing with internationals did bring out the best in Peter and he had a great game at Derwent Park that day.

In the same team as Peter were some of the biggest names of that era and he was fortunate enough to play with Peter Smethurst, Eric Prescott (whose son Steve would go on to be a star in the Super League era), Geoff Fletcher, Paul Charlton, Phil Kitchen, John Bevan, Dave Smith and Ray Wilkins. The referee was Peter Geraghty.

On a warm afternoon, more than 1,000 fans were there to see the Cumbrian team win 34-22 with the beneficiary fittingly scoring three tries.

Peter's outstanding performance further alerted professional clubs to his potential. Wigan, Leigh and Barrow had all expressed an interest in signing him, but in the dressing room he was approached by Tom Mitchell, Workington Town's chairman and certainly the most influential figure in the club's history. Workington had been interested in Peter for two years, but he had preferred to stay in the

Headline news when Peter turned professional

Peter signs on — after two years

amateur game. Tom had been impressed by what he had seen and he made it very clear that he wanted to sign Peter - so much so that he went to visit him in Broughton that same evening. He obviously liked the idea of having two Gorleys in a developing pack and, no doubt inspired by Les's success, Peter signed professional for Workington Town. Wigan and Leigh had been in the hunt for his signature, but he decided to join his local team.

Thus ended Workington's two year bid to sign one of Cumberland amateur Rugby League's most promising forwards and best goal-kickers.

Peter in action for Workington Town against Huddersfield
(Photo: Courtesy Robert Gate)

2. Going to Town

It was 1975 and Peter was 24 - a relatively late starter in the professional game, but he would soon make up for lost time.

He had very much enjoyed his time in the amateur game and he left it with only one real regret - he hadn't represented his country although this was through no fault of his own and no lack of ability on his part. Looking back, he feels that he could probably have turned professional earlier but that he didn't is testimony to how much he enjoyed playing locally at Broughton. Perhaps, Peter acknowledges, he was a little blinkered and lacking in ambition in his younger days. He would certainly have enjoyed an even longer and more distinguished professional career if he had signed earlier.

On the other hand, had he done so, he would have missed one of his finest hours in the amateur game which occurred shortly before he signed for Town when he captained Broughton in the Cumberland Cup final against in-form Egremont. He recalls that it was a tough match - as all cup finals should be, of course - and at half-time Broughton led 4-0 thanks to two penalties from Peter, a recognised and accomplished goalkicker.

An abiding memory of that match is the tussle Peter and his mates had with Louis Shepherd. Then at the veteran stage, Louis had been a professional principally with Whitehaven - although he had also played a few games for Workington - and he had the reputation of being able to look after himself. He was a tough customer who was not averse to dishing it out. Peter and his good friend Alan Varty who later also signed for Town came in for some treatment and found themselves with bloodied mouths - an occupational hazard for hard men in a hard game. Eventually, after one foul too many on Alan, the referee's patience was exhausted and Louis Shepherd was sent off. Broughton went on to win 23-0, scoring 19 points in the last 20 minutes. This was the club's first trophy and a source of immense satisfaction to Peter and the team of predominantly local lads.

The man-of-the-match award went to full-back Ron Fletcher but Peter's contribution - two tries and four goals - was immense. Broughton's other tries were scored by Edmund Routledge, Dave

Collister - who would eventually join Peter at Workington - and Jackie Newall.

Peter was delighted to receive the trophy from George Nixon, the secretary of Whitehaven RLFC, and a barrel of beer provided by Eric Stephenson, landlord of the Volunteer Inn, helped the team to celebrate in a suitable manner.

The inspiration behind the win was undoubtedly player-coach Jackie Newall, a scrum-half who had served Workington for 11 years from 1963. Jackie was another hard man - "he never took a backward step," recalls Peter - and he led by example, taking knocks, sometimes needlessly. Peter remembers a match at Wath Brow when he fired out a pass to his coach and immediately wished he hadn't. All he could do was apologise as Jackie returned to the land of the living aided by the trainer's magic sponge. Jackie knew this was part and parcel of the game and so he bore no grudges, but he did suggest that Peter might think a little more carefully before passing next time.

There is no doubt that Peter was a star of the amateur game and contemporary newspaper reports wrote of his prowess as a goal-kicker and points scorer. In one sequence of five league games he scored 57 points and his career was studded with many other outstanding performances such as scoring three tries and six goals in a 39-15 win over Grasslot, two tries and six goals in a 45-0 win over Greenbank and 22 points out of 28 in a victory over Wath Brow. At this time, forwards were not renowned for scoring.

However, Peter was to leave all that behind when he travelled a few miles down the A66 to sign professional forms at Derwent Park.

He joined at a good time in Workington's history. In the 1950s Town had had a team to be feared which was one of the best in the league. The club won the championship in 1951, a mere six years after its formation and three times in that decade West Cumbrians made the long pilgrimage to Wembley once, in 1952, bringing home the much coveted Challenge Cup. There was also some success in the early 1960s when Town won the now defunct Western Championship beating Widnes in the final. However, later in the 1960s and in the early 1970s decline set in and the club's fortunes - and attendances - slumped. Workington remained difficult to beat at home but Derwent Park was no longer an impregnable fortress and Town struggled for positive results from their long journeys to Lancashire and Yorkshire.

When the decision was taken to divide the 30-strong Rugby League competition into two divisions, the Workington club were not placed high enough at the end of the final single-division season, 1972-1973, so found itself in the Second Division. The next two years were ones of consolidation. In each season the team finished in fifth position in the table, just missing out by one place on promotion. At the same time the club started to redevelop its cup pedigree - in both seasons, for example, Workington defeated St Helens in the Lancashire Cup, once at Knowsley Road.

Paul Charlton

There were definite signs that a revival was not too far away. Paul Charlton, a rugby league legend in Cumbria and a highly respected figure wherever the game is played, had rejoined the club as player-coach. Paul's career had started at an amateur club. He then joined Workington in 1960, and made his first team debut in 1961.

He had earned a reputation as an outstanding and adventurous full-back with an amazing flair for scoring tries. In October 1969 Salford, then in the ascendancy and rugby league's 'big spenders', tempted Workington with a cheque for £13,000 and, on what Tom Mitchell later described as the saddest day of his time at Workington, Paul moved south. He prospered in a Salford team full of stars which became renowned for its ability to thrill supporters with an exciting brand of attacking rugby. He set a new record of tries in a season for a full-back with the wonderful tally of 33 in the 1972-73 season but this was of no consolation to Workington fans, still upset by the departure of their prize asset.

The 1975-76 season saw both the return of Charlton and the emergence of Peter Gorley. There was a feeling that the return of a big star from the 1960s would herald an upturn in fortunes, and so it proved. Paul, respected and admired, proved inspirational on and off the field and he helped to mould talented players into a good team.

He holds the appearances record for Workington Town with 415+4 in his two spells with the club.

Peter recalls the names of some of his team mates at that time - Paul, Eddie Bowman, Arnold Walker, Alan Banks, Ralph Calvin, Ian Wright, John Risman and, of course, his brother Les - "all good players" is Peter's accurate verdict.

Eddie Bowman joined Town from neighbours Whitehaven in 1970 with Workington forward Dennis Martin following his brother Bill to the Recreation Ground as part of the deal. Eddie had made his name as a running second-rower with his home-town club, evoking memories of former 'Haven great Dick Huddart, and he proved a great capture for Workington, appearing almost 200 times for the club. He developed his skills as a ball handler and he later switched to prop forward, a position in which he also excelled. This change of role enabled Peter and Les to form a fraternal pairing in the Town second-row. Eddie was at the top of his form when he appeared four times down under for Great Britain in the 1977 World Cup. In 1978 he moved to Leigh, and he later transferred to Wigan where he finished his career.

Arnold Walker, universally known as 'Boxer', also played for both West Cumbrian clubs, but in a different order to Eddie. Although born in Whitehaven and a product of the famous Kells amateur club, he joined Workington in 1971 and played much of his career with Eddie at Derwent Park. He, too, played nearly 200 games and he was a brilliant scrum-half as well as a drop-goal expert registering 35, more than anyone else for Workington. After his match-winning Lancashire Cup final display in 1977, when he dropped two goals, all-time great Alex Murphy described him as the best uncapped scrum-half in the game. The magazine *Open Rugby* rated him even more highly and, at one stage in Boxer's career, placed him at the very top of their prestigious world ratings. He played his last match for Workington in the 1979 Lancashire Cup Final and it cost his home town team £30,000 to sign him in 1980. He went on to represent Great Britain against New Zealand after starring for Cumbria when they beat the Kiwis, but his career was curtailed following an horrific neck injury sustained in a home match against Hull Kingston Rovers in October 1981 which led to the game being abandoned. The score was 5-5 at the time, and Walker had scored all Whitehaven's points.

Alan Banks was the hooker during Peter's time at Workington. At first he was a patient understudy to Howard Allen, having made his debut in the 1969-70 season, but he began to establish himself three years later and he became a fixture in the team, serving the club with distinction for 12 years - indeed, only four forwards have made more appearances for Workington than his record of 279+6. He provided his team mates with a good supply of possession on a regular basis and was lively in loose play. Like Allen before him, he was an underrated ball winner. After his time at Derwent Park he went to play for Blackpool Borough.

Ralph Calvin was a tough, no-nonsense forward from Whitehaven who served Workington from 1968 to 1982 and he never let the club down when called into action. He represented his county on five occasions in the now defunct County Championship. At the end of his career he followed in the footsteps of many before him by moving to his home town club and he became chairman of Whitehaven in the late 1990s.

Ian Wright signed from Cockermouth RUFC in 1966 as a stand-off but he rapidly gained a reputation as a consistent, try-scoring centre. He scored three tries on his Derwent Park debut for Town's 'A' team and he was the club's top try scorer in his first season. Despite injury problems, he would repeat this feat in seven subsequent seasons and he went on to total 168 tries in his 13-year career, the most valuable of which was probably the one he scored in the 1977 Lancashire Cup Final against Wigan. Only legendary Great Britain winger Ike Southward has touched down more times for Workington. Ian also gained selection for Cumberland as well as for the Great Britain under-24 team, scoring twice on his only appearance, and many good judges consider he was unlucky not to gain full honours, suggesting that he might have been more fortunate had he played for a glamorous club.

John Risman's name evokes great memories among older Workington followers for he is the son of the great Gus Risman, the mercurial Welshman who was so instrumental in the club's early successes. Gus led the club to Championship and Challenge Cup

11

glory in the early 1950s and he held the club record for most points in a career until Iain MacCorquodale broke it in the 1970s. Rugby league was definitely in the Risman family's blood because John's brother Bev played for Leigh and Leeds, starring as a goal-kicking full-back in one of Headingley's finest teams.

John lost little by comparison. Having joined Workington from Carlisle RUFC in 1971 he played more than 200 games in a 10-year career and was good enough to represent Cumbria and Wales as well as featuring in two Lancashire Cup Finals. He was very versatile, being able to play at centre, wing and full-back with equal aplomb, and Tom Mitchell's description of him as "strong and daunting" was based on his defensive capabilities. When he left Workington, he played briefly for Blackpool Borough and then in 1980 joined the newly formed Fulham club which had a team of northern-based players to entertain the game's new fans in West London. He ended his career with a second spell at the seaside for Blackpool before appearing for Carlisle.

Because these players were established at the club when Peter arrived, he had good role models to help him when he broke into the Workington team.

Workington debut

At this time Workington had no 'A' team so there was no chance of a new player being brought gradually into the professional game. Peter was thrown in at the deep end with a debut as substitute in a match against Blackpool Borough. It was, he acknowledges, something of a big step - an ordeal even.

The game has changed. Seaside trips to Blackpool for rugby league have become a thing of the past. Many fans consider this is a shame. Certainly they were once popular away visits.

Blackpool Borough's first season was 1954-55 and after starting at the southern end of the town the club settled at Borough Park, a neat little stadium not far from the Tower and the bright lights of the famous Golden Mile. Life was a struggle with only occasional highlights such as the 1976-77 John Player Trophy Final appearance in which Smiler Allen featured and a solitary season in Division One.

As the game became unsustainable on the Fylde Coast and the stadium fell into disrepair, a nomadic existence followed as the team went to play at Springfield Park, Wigan (now itself no longer in use), Chorley and Trafford. It seems a long time since supporters used to study the fixture list in the hope that their team's away fixture at Blackpool would coincide with the pleasant spring weather or, better still, would be in September or October so that the trip could be combined with a visit to the illuminations later.

Peter's first appearance in Workington's first team was one such match on the 'Lancashire Riviera' on 2 November 1975. The illuminations had just ended and Blackpool was taking on a deserted air as the visitors had left and the hoteliers were off to sunnier climes for a well earned rest.

His earliest memory of first team rugby was an attempted tackle on Cliff Darbyshire, Blackpool's scrum-half, whose hand-off left Peter sitting rather sheepishly in the Borough Park mud - not the greatest of starts. However, he was able to begin his career with a victory as Workington won 25-8.

Workington: Charlton; Risman, Atkinson, Wright, MacCorquodale; Nicholson Walker; Gibbs, Banks, Henney, Bowman, L. Gorley, Pattinson. Subs: Marland, P. Gorley.

Blackpool Borough: Reynolds; Johnson, Haigh, Heritage, Pitman; Marsh, Darbyshire; Bate, Martland, Hamilton, Hurst, Secker, Seddon. Subs: Greenough, Hallas

Workington's tries came from Atkinson, Wright, Charlton, Les Gorley and MacCorquodale who also kicked five goals. Johnson and Hamilton scored tries for Blackpool, while Marsh added a goal.

Peter began to settle into the first team and he didn't have to wait too long for his first try which helped to beat York 29-7 at Derwent Park in December. He took a pass from Alan Banks and sprinted in from about 25 yards to touch down at the river end and join his brother on the list of try scorers - Les scored a hat-trick in the match. He also made up for an earlier goal-kicking failure. He had an outstanding kicking record at amateur level, once scoring 15 goals in a game and his captain must have been aware of this when he asked Peter to have a go. He remembers his effort finishing up nearer the corner flag than the goal posts, and it seemed to be that goal-kicking had ceased to be his forte. In fact he didn't kick any goals at all during his time at Derwent Park; it was probably considered that Iain MacCorquodale was a better candidate for the job even though he wasn't playing that day.

Workington Town: Marland; Risman, Atkinson, Nicholson, Elwin; McMillan, Walker; Gibbs, Banks, Bowman, L. Gorley, P. Gorley, Pattinson. Sub: McCracken.

York: Banks; Barends, Day, Wilson, Marshall; Harkin G. Smith; Clawson, Handforth, S. Cooper, Rhodes, Bennett, Hetherington. Subs: A Trialist, C. Smith.

As well as the brothers' four-try haul, Bowman, Atkinson and Risman scored tries while Elwin kicked four goals. Scrum-half Smith scored a try for York and Hetherington kicked two goals.

Only 582 people turned out to watch, although interest increased as Town went on to improve on their position of sixth in the table.

Although he was missing that afternoon, Iain MacCorquodale became a scoring phenomenon with Workington; no one has scored more goals (810) or points (1,802) for the club, and it is very difficult to envisage his records being broken. One of the few non-Cumbrians in the side - he was born in Oldham - he became disenchanted with a lack of first team opportunities at Salford having joined them from Waterloo RUFC and he moved to Derwent Park in 1972. He began to pile up the points immediately and in his first season broke the club record for goals in a game, kicking 11 against Blackpool Borough and receiving the congratulations of his coach, Ike Southward - the man whose record he had broken. His consistency - and good fortune with injury - led to his scoring in 46 consecutive matches between 1975 and 1977 and he played in every match in 1977-78 and 1978-79, breaking Gus Risman's record for points scored in the former season. To prove he was not just a goal-kicking machine, he scored over 70 tries as a left winger to become a key man in Town's last golden age.

Clear progress was made as the season moved into its second half and thanks to some excellent performances as well as some good press coverage; Peter's efforts began to be noticed. During the match at Thrum Hall, Halifax in February, which was always a daunting prospect, it was reported that: "Workington's best were the

Gorley brothers, Les and Peter, in the second row..." Peter made a try for John Risman in a narrow 12-10 win. Two weeks later in another close game against New Hunslet, local reporter Eric Easterbrook wrote that Peter would have headed the list if medals had been given out for effort. Playing at loose-forward, his great tackling stood out and, in only his 14th first-team game, he seemed to be doing the work of three men. The match, which marked Dave Collister's Workington debut, was won 18-14, and a mere two months after the York game, the attendance had increased to 1,252.

Peter's first season ended in great style with a win at Bramley by 14-5 which secured third place in Division Two and promotion. Bramley, featuring stalwarts such as Jack Austin who had enjoyed success at Castleford and would go on to further success under Peter Fox at Bradford, were never easy to beat at home, and it was a happy Workington squad which broke its journey home in Penrith to, in Peter's words, "paint the town red" (although the Workington colours of blue and white might have been more suitable). It must have been an even happier group which continued its journey past Keswick and Bassenthwaite Lake contemplating its triumph and, perhaps, the greater challenges which were to lie ahead.

Curiously for a club whose reputation had been built on hugely successful efforts at home and sometimes tamer performances elsewhere, the promotion success was based on an unbeaten away record while four visitors - champions Barrow, Hull, Leigh and Rochdale Hornets won on the Cumbrian coast. However, it was third-time-lucky and the aim of promotion had been achieved. Peter and Workington Town were ready for the big time.

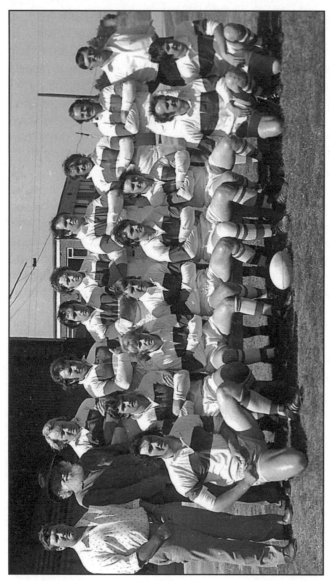

Workington Town 1976
Back:
I. Southward (coach),
T. Mitchell (chairman),
L. Gorley,
R. Calvin,
I. Wright,
P. Gorley,
J. Mills,
E. Bowman,
J. Risman,
J. Atkinson (director)
Front:
D. Collister,
H. Henney, A. Walker,
P. Charlton,
A. Banks,
D. McMillan,
H. Marland,
I. MacCorquodale.

(Photo: *Workington Times & Star*)

3. Up Town boys

It was to be very different in the rarefied atmosphere of the top division. At this time a four-up, four-down system of promotion and relegation was used and records show invariably that at least two of the previous season's promoted teams failed to survive, so no-one at Derwent Park had any illusions about the size of the challenge.

During Peter's time there Workington Town gained well-deserved respect built largely on redoubtable displays at home just as good Town teams had done in the past. There was a return to the good old days when the best most visiting teams could hope for, apart from the hosts' Cumbrian hospitality, was a chance to admire the excellent Cumbrian scenery - if the fells and lakes weren't shrouded in mist - and to enjoy a pleasant refreshment stop en route.

Peter played three seasons successfully at the highest level with Workington between 1976 and 1979 – a fine record considering the fate of many promoted teams. The team completed those seasons in 12th, 11th and ninth positions and it appeared in each season's Lancashire Cup Final. Peter was certainly a vital member of the side, playing 105 times and he was very well supported by the players mentioned in the previous chapter who would become familiar names to those supporters who watched First Division rugby league at that time.

The Workington team of the late 1970s was not as successful in the league as that of the 1950s - although comparison is very difficult, because there was no two division system in place in the 1950s - but it surpassed the efforts of previous teams by reaching the final of the Lancashire Cup for the first time. While in the Second Division it had warmed up by reaching three consecutive semi-finals and now promotion to the First Division seemed to breed the confidence needed to go one step further. The first match began a hat-trick of final appearances for Peter and it is not surprising that many of his best memories centre on this competition which, sadly, no longer takes place.

The first Lancashire Cup Final of the sequence on 30 October 1976 was to end in disappointment. Having reached the final by beating Swinton, Blackpool Borough and Warrington (in a replay) all at home, Town were pitted against Widnes at Central Park, Wigan. Widnes were in the process of establishing themselves as the Cup Kings and, plagued by memories of a heavy Wembley defeat at the hands of St Helens six months earlier, were well focused on the first final of the new season. Workington were going well, however, and were stunning when they beat Warrington by the very impressive margin of 26-15 in the semi-final in front of a large, enthusiastic Cumbrian crowd. The players were inspired by Jim Mills who was having a 'sabbatical' in Cumbria somewhat away from the media spotlight, following his involvement in a stamping incident while playing for Wales.

Workington played well at Wigan, but they did not enjoy the best of fortune and Peter recalls that with better luck the trophy could have been on its way up the M6. Widnes won by five points, but to say there was a little doubt about the clinching try would be something of an understatement. Widnes's flying winger Stuart Wright got his fingertips to a bouncing ball very close to the dead ball line - but on which side of the line? Photographic evidence strongly suggests that he was behind it when he reached the ball and, to compound Town's disappointment, Ray Dutton's touchline conversion went in off the post. It was a sickening blow from which Workington did not recover.

In his autobiography, Tom Mitchell says that he rang Stuart Wright to ask about the try and Stuart was honest enough to admit that an error had been made in his favour. The mistake cost Workington five points - the margin of defeat. Widnes won 16-11.

Workington had actually taken the lead after an excellent penalty goal from Iain MacCorquodale who also converted Ray Wilkins's try, but they could register no more tries while, crucially, Mick George also touched down for Widnes. MacCorquodale finished with four goals, whereas Widnes's Dutton kicked five including a drop-goal. The Chemics' other point came from a drop-goal from scrum-half Reg Bowden.

Widnes had had the good fortune and this, coupled with their greater experience, had tipped the balance their way. Workington's players were understandably disappointed, but they had enjoyed the big match atmosphere and they felt the experience would help them in the future. They were confident this would not be their last final.

Workington: Charlton; Collister, Wilkins, Wright, MacCorquodale; Lauder, Walker; Mills, Banks, Calvin, Bowman, L. Gorley, Pattinson. Subs: P. Gorley

Widnes: Dutton; Wright, Aspey, George, Prescott; Eckersley, Bowden; Ramsey, Elwell, Nelson, Adams, Dearden, Laughton.

The referee, as he was for all Workington's final appearances, was Billy Thompson of Huddersfield who later went on to become one of the more entertaining speakers on the after-dinner circuit.

At the end of the season it was perhaps some small consolation to Town fans that the team had done the double over Widnes in the league but the silverware was firmly ensconced at Naughton Park.

The following season, doubtless spurred on by memories of the previous season's final, Workington went on the Lancashire Cup trail again. Having beaten Salford in Cumbria in the first round, everyone at the club was delighted to be given the opportunity to wreak revenge on Widnes and they duly did, beating the holders 8-6 at home. Next up was St Helens, erstwhile Lancashire Cup kings and a club anxious to regain its standing in the competition.

The game, played at tea time on a Wednesday in late September because Derwent Park had no floodlights at that time, holds fond memories for Peter and I, too, clearly recall events surrounding the fixture - although perhaps not quite as fondly. At the time I was studying German at Newcastle University and was preparing to spend a year in Austria as a language assistant. I was scheduled to travel to Vienna the following Sunday and for a couple of days before the match I had been on Tyneside, ostensibly tying up some loose ends, but in fact more concerned with farewell drinks.

The cup tie was to be my last match for a while and I was determined not to miss it. It was a fine, sunny morning as I stood on the Westgate Road in west end of Newcastle, thumb raised, waiting for a 'friend' I had not yet met to take me to Carlisle and maybe even beyond to the coast.

I had left myself plenty of time and this was one of my more successful hitching expeditions. Lifts came quickly, and I arrived in Workington at about 2.30pm, a full three hours before kick off. This left plenty of time to explore all the nooks and crannies and to find something to eat before the protagonists locked horns.

Because the match was so close to my departure for Europe I didn't feel I could take any chances for the trip back to Lancashire after the match so I had booked a seat, one way, on a coach which I had to locate after the game. The trip home, in near silence, was miserable, and I remember thinking that it would be a long time before I would be able to see Saints make amends for that evening.

The reason for the gloom and despondency was Town's 5-4 win in a cup tie long on passion, commitment and skill but short on tries. Iain MacCorquodale was unusually off form with his kicking and missed all his kicks in the first half, which left Saints 2-0 up at the break. Workington endured some nervous moments as visiting winger Les Jones was held just short and his fellow wing man Roy Mathias touched down, but was adjudged to have put a foot in touch. Two goals put the home team ahead 4-2, but in the 71st minute visiting full-back Geoff Pimblett equalised with a penalty.

Both teams had kicked two penalty goals and a draw was looking likely. It was inevitably left to the expert, Boxer Walker, to drop the goal which made the difference. Peter recalls a drop-goal attempt by Saints' Harry Pinner - later to be one of his best friends at Knowsley Road - which would have tied the game, sailing narrowly wide. With a replay at Knowsley Road, Saints would have fancied their chances but it was not to be. I can still picture the joy of the home fans, one of whom, having spotted a particularly crestfallen Saints forward, invited me in his broad Cumbrian accent, to "just look at the expression on that Chisnall's face" as I tried to sneak away, as disappointed as the players.

One of Peter's mates in the Workington pack that evening was Derek Watts who had made his name in a fearsome Leigh forward line and he was voted 'man-of-the-match'. However, it was very gratifying for Peter to hear in the bar afterwards that many good judges thought that he had been the top performer. Perhaps his efforts that day had been duly noted by visiting officials, for two years later he moved to St Helens.

Memories of that match also prompts Peter to mention another of his good friends and a hard, tough opponent who never gave less than 100 per cent on a rugby field. George Nicholls starred at Widnes before moving to St Helens in the early 1970s. It speaks volumes for George's tenacity and ability that, later that season, he won the Lance Todd Trophy at Wembley despite being on the losing side against Leeds. "It was always hard to win with George in the team against you," says Peter of a man for whom he has the greatest respect.

Town therefore moved into their second consecutive Lancashire Cup Final. Their opponents this time were to be Wigan on the equivalent Saturday to the defeat against Widnes. Peter and his mates were prepared for the big game at Wilderspool Stadium.

If you are based on the Cumbrian coast and you reach the final of a competition for predominantly Lancashire teams, there's an unavoidable problem in finding a well situated neutral venue. A glance at a good road map reveals that Warrington is not between Workington and Wigan. Nevertheless this did not deter the thousands of fans who made their way south that day and the masses of blue and white around the ground assured the players that they would have plenty of support. It is said that every coach and minibus in Workington was used to carry supporters and the demand was so great that additional transport was brought over Dunmail Raise from Ambleside.

What else could provide Workington with motivation? Before the game they received a boost from their opponents when Wigan sold Bill Francis to arch rivals St Helens. Francis was a clever play-making stand-off and his new team played some sensational rugby that season, reaching Wembley. His presence at Warrington that day could well have made a difference, although, of course, we will never know. At the very least, feels Peter, it would have increased Wigan's chances of success.

Wigan inadvertently provided further motivation when the Town camp discovered an example of gross over-confidence - some might say arrogance - before the match. The players were so certain they would win that they had organised a match-winning celebration for that evening. In addition it was alleged that one of the Wigan players had placed a bet on his team to win. Ike Southward, Workington's coach, must have been thankful to the Wiganers for making his pre-match motivational task easier.

If any more incentive were needed, the charismatic Tom Mitchell had promised to take the team to Benidorm for a week if they won the cup. Peter had never been abroad before and neither had some of the other members of the team.

Workington's front-row forward Ken Groves was ruled out so the pack was in need of some adjustment. Eddie Bowman moved up to prop, with the Gorleys in the second row and Billy Pattinson at loose-forward, while Ian Hartley was substitute forward.

The match, of course, has gone down in Workington's history because they did, indeed, win, 16-13, to bring back the Lancashire Cup for the first time. There were heroes aplenty. Ian Wright scored the first try after 10 minutes, finishing a powerful break from Les Gorley and Ray Wilkins scored the second try, this time completing a break by Peter after Boxer had created the space. Town were indebted to the great kicking of Iain MacCorquodale, particularly in the second half when he landed three towering penalties to ease his team away from Wigan and Boxer's morale boosting drop-goals.

Peter played a large part in the triumph. In the *News of the World* Alan Gaskell wrote: "Yet neither Walker nor MacCorquodale could have grabbed their share of glory but for the powerful Workington pack with international Eddie Bowman, hooker Alan Banks and the Gorley brothers, Peter and Les, outstanding." In the *Sunday Telegraph* Michael Crossley observed: "The two Gorley brothers were also in unquenchable mood in the second-row, Workington's first half tries by Wright and Wilkins stemming from their storming bursts."

Wigan actually outscored Workington three tries to two, Dave Willicombe, Bill Ashurst and Jimmy Nulty all touching down, with winger Green Vigo having a try ruled out, but superior goal-kicking, team spirit and a huge desire to win saw Workington through. They were even able to resist the loss late in the game of inspirational full-back Paul Charlton with a leg injury. At the end of the contest the pitch was transformed into a sea of blue and white as the jubilant Cumbrian fans mobbed their heroes. Peter said: "The supporters were great - they tackled us harder than Wigan when the hooter sounded and they ran onto the pitch. It's just great to win a final like this and it's the highlight of my professional career."

When Tom Mitchell entered the field he kept to his pre-match promise and headed straight to Peter. He had said that if Workington could win the cup he would present Peter with one of his trademark fedora hats and, true to his word, he did. Tom said: "It has taken 32 years and all the time I've been in charge of the team. But it's been well worth waiting for." Ike Southward was equally delighted with his first trophy win as a player or coach. "Get that cup over here," he shouted in the dressing room after the game. "I've waited 22 years to sample that champagne after playing in losing sides at Wembley and in the Championship Final." Twenty two years was a slight exaggeration on Ike's part, but there is no doubt that he deserved his celebratory drink.

Peter thought very highly of Tom, as did the other players. Nicknamed 'The Godfather', Tom was instrumental in ensuring the Workington club was accepted into the RFL after the Second World War, and much of Town's success in the early days can be attributed to his tireless work. To everyone within the game, he *was* Workington Town. Instantly recognisable with luxuriant beard and headgear, T.M. was very well respected and in 1976 he was elected a life member of the Rugby Football League. He died in September 1999 and was a huge loss to the game everywhere, not just in Cumbria. Peter and Les were greatly honoured when Tom's son asked them to be bearers at his father's funeral.

Back at the Lancashire Cup Final, the Wigan contingent was hugely disappointed - it was their second cup defeat of the week following a Floodlit Trophy loss at Hull Kingston Rovers - but they accepted the loss in a sporting manner. Wigan's Cumbrian forward, Bob Blackwood, was one of the first to offer his congratulations, while coach Vince Karalius said: "We just weren't good enough. We were just individuals. We didn't do the right things... The only consoling factor is that the cup has gone to Workington and to Tom Mitchell who is one of my best pals." Tom, for his part, was philosophical and said to his great friend: "Vinty, you will just have to get used to it and read all about it in tomorrow's papers. They will

Tom Mitchell, Paul Charlton, Arnie Walker and Peter Gorley, with the Cup
(Photo: Courtesy Robert Gate)

report that we got more points on the scoreboard than you did."
Once the game is over, you can never argue with the scoreboard.

It was Workington's first trophy since the Western Championship
victory in 1962-63, and a great day in the history of the club.

Workington: Charlton; Collister, Risman, Wright, MacCorquodale;
Wilkins, Walker; Watts, Banks, Bowman, L. Gorley, P. Gorley,
Pattinson. Sub: Atkinson.

Wigan: Swann; Vigo, Willicombe, Davies, Hornby; Taylor, Nulty; Hogan, Aspinall, Irving, Ashurst, Melling, Blackwood.

Subs: Burke, Regan.

The players had a holiday in Benidorm at the end of the season, paid for by Tom Mitchell, to celebrate their cup win. Eddie Bowman recalls the week: "We had a great time and spent a lot of time in former Oldham player Dave Parker's pub. One day we started arm wrestling and there was nobody could beat Peter. A few Spaniards saw us doing the arm wrestling and in the next few hours they were bringing Spaniards from all over the place to take Peter on. Nobody all week could get near Peter so he left Benidorm as champion. He was a pleasure to play with and a guy to be out with socially."

Boxer Walker remembers another incident from the trip. It was a typically hot, sunny Spanish afternoon when, while partaking of some much needed liquid refreshment, Peter began talking to a local with a huge motorcycle. The mean machine was large enough to seat three people and Peter persuaded the rider to give himself and his friend a ride.

The bike, with the rider at the front, Arnie in the middle and Peter at the rear, roared off down Benidorm's main street. Its owner was clearly keen to impress. However, recalled the intrepid scrum-half, Peter found the estimated speed of 100 mph. to be a little too slow and he urged the rider to go ever faster. In order to give the Spaniard the opportunity to demonstrate his skills, Peter leaned forward from the back and put his hands across the rider's eyes. Boxer had never experienced anything like it and when the ordeal was over he was shaking like a leaf - in fact, the trembling was so severe, he couldn't lift his pint for another two hours. On the other hand Peter, adrenaline coursing through his veins, simply beamed at his 'marra' and said, "Come on - we'll have another go!"

Despite all the events on the end-of-season trip, the players survived for another Lancashire Cup campaign the next season.

Third final

Unfortunately Peter's third Lancashire Cup Final appearance in early October 1978 ended in disappointment, again at the hands of

Widnes. The road to the final began with a rematch of the previous season's final, Town winning 14-2 at home, and their reward was a bye into the semi-final (only 14 clubs entered the competition) where a tough looking assignment against Salford at the Willows was in prospect. Workington squeezed through 9-8 to qualify to meet Widnes once more. Wigan again was the venue.

This time, unlike two years previously, Peter was given a starting place in the second-row and his brother was on the bench. As in the previous encounter ultimately there was little to choose between the teams but Workington certainly began more strongly and the first try arrived after only two minutes, courtesy of Ray Wilkins. Building on the great start, Boxer made a try for Iain MacCorquodale shortly after and once Les Gorley, a replacement for the injured Billy Pattinson, had stormed through for a converted try before the interval, Town held an 11-5 lead at half time. When a second half goal extended Workington's lead to 13-5 with only 13 minutes left confidence was high but, thanks to player-coach Doug Laughton's second try, Widnes reduced the lead and set up a grandstand finish. Widnes, in the eyes of some onlookers, stole the cup with a try seven minutes from time which was brilliantly converted by young full-back Mick Burke. Those who say lightning never strikes twice were forced to think again. Once more Stuart Wright proved to be the thorn in Town's flesh as he scored a crucial try with an element of controversy about it. The try arrived as a result of a break from Mal Aspey who put his wing man over in the corner but the Workington camp felt that Paul Charlton might well have been able to have made the tackle but for some shirt pulling which went unnoticed. The teams that day were:

Workington Town: Charlton; Collister, Risman, Wilkins, MacCorquodale; McMillan, Walker; Beverley, Banks, Bowman, P. Gorley, Blackwood, Pattinson. Sub: L. Gorley

Widnes: Eckersley; Wright, Aspey, George, Burke; Hughes, Bowden; Mills, Elwell, Shaw, Adams, Dearden, Laughton. Subs: Hull, Woods.

So, Workington were defeated, but far from disgraced. Arguably the better team, Workington did not really deserve to lose. A measure of Town's contribution was that, despite being on the losing side, Boxer was the man-of-the-match. This was the second

Workington 24 September 1978 versus Bramley in the John Player Trophy at
Derwent Park. The same team played in the Lancashire Cup Final.
Back: I. Rudd, W. Pattinson, D. Collister, R. Blackwood, E. Bowman,
H. Beverley, P. Gorley, J. Risman, L. Gorley,
Front: D. McMillan, R. Wilkins, P. Charlton, A. Walker, A. Banks,
I. MacCorquodale. (Photo: Courtesy Robert Gate)

successive award for the brilliant scrum-half following his nomination
against Wigan the year before. It was clear the team was still good
enough to challenge for honours.

Sadly, the next trophies the club was to win - the Second Division
championship and Divisional Premiership - did not find their way to
Derwent Park until 1994. Even more sadly, in the Super League era,
it is extremely hard to see where Workington's next trophies at the
top level will come from.

Peter's proud record was three Lancashire Cup finals in three
years, three more than such great players as Gus Risman, Billy
Ivison, Ike Southward and Brian Edgar achieved with the same club.

Cup ties seemed to bring out the best in Workington, so how did
Peter fare in other competitions in the same era? The team did not
emulate their final appearances in the other competitions but their
cup pedigree inspired some good runs. In 1976-77, for instance,
Town reached the quarter-final stages of both the John Player
Trophy and the Challenge Cup and even though they were favoured
with a home tie on each occasion, both games were lost in
disappointing fashion. Certainly the John Player defeat by Second

27

Division Blackpool Borough was especially hard to take. Blackpool won 11-5 and went on to their fondly remembered final appearance. It must have been particularly galling that Smiler Allen, on his return to Derwent Park, was Borough's match winner with two of his trademark tries, perfected during his long Workington career.

When Leeds visited in the third round of the Challenge Cup, some West Cumbrians had Wembley in sight again. A visit was overdue - it had been a long time since 1958 and Workington's home record was good enough to give grounds for optimism. Sadly, the team didn't play well enough, Leeds won a close game 8-2, and went on to lift the trophy.

Workington were involved in a rarity in 1978 - a marathon of a Challenge Cup tie covering three matches. Town and Castleford drew 8-8 in Cumbria and, by an amazing coincidence; the result was exactly the same when the teams met at Wheldon Road in the replay. The two teams had to reconvene at Wigan where Castleford won 20-13 to move into the quarter-final.

On a visit home from Europe I remember talking to my cousin, a fellow Knowsley Road regular, and he was bringing me up to date on rugby league. He had been to the second replay and was singing the praises of Peter Gorley, the younger of the two powerhouse brothers in the Workington pack. He thought that he would fit in well at Knowsley Road. In view of future events, there might have been a more official delegation from Knowsley Road beside the River Douglas that evening.

The last cup tie during Peter's time at Workington was in the 1979 Challenge Cup and, perhaps fittingly, it was against Widnes. Naughton Park was nobody's idea of an ideal cup tie venue (except for Widnes, of course) and victory went to the home side by 12-5. Perhaps the only consolation was that Workington had lost to the eventual winners.

4. Consolidation time

Away from cup competitions, Peter and his team mates began to bridge the gap between the Second and First Divisions most effectively, improving their final position with each successive season. Although never looking likely to challenge for league honours, Workington took some notable scalps, particularly at Derwent Park, and they could usually be relied upon to give a good account of themselves whatever the opposition.

A measure of the team's progress came early in the 1976-77 season when Leeds were beaten 18-3 at Derwent Park. Peter scored the opening try to set Town on the way but the highlight was a spectacular 90-yard interception try from prolific centre Ian Wright. A crowd of 2,508 saw Workington register their second win out of their first three games to move into second place in the First Division table, behind Castleford. St Helens, Wigan, Bradford and Leeds were all absent from the top six at that stage - a far cry from the Big Four's closed shop which seems to exist in 21st century Super League.

Building on this start, Workington finished 12th. Only five visiting teams left Town's ground with maximum points but, conversely, Workington managed only four victories on their travels. A glance at the final table shows they were only one place above relegated Rochdale Hornets, but they had a comfortable five-point cushion at the end of the season.

Peter certainly played his part in the club's successful transition. He played on 38 occasions that season, failing to feature in only three matches, and he registered four tries.

The 1977-78 season again saw Town survive in the top flight, although at 12-0 down to Hull KR at Derwent Park in a late season 'must-win' game, prospects looked bleak. Peter again scored the first try which sparked a Workington recovery, and the 23-18 victory ensured the team's salvation.

The club's, and Peter's, efforts largely mirrored those of the previous season - Town lost only four times at home, but only two victories - at Wakefield and Salford - were recorded away. This time Peter missed a mere two games, playing 38 times and scoring six tries, although he wasn't top of the appearances chart this time, Alan Banks and Iain MacCorquodale being ever-present.

It was a particularly successful foray into Yorkshire which provided Peter with his favourite memory of top flight league football with Workington. Trips to Leeds are never easy. Headingley, with its impressive facilities, is an imposing and perhaps somewhat daunting - yet at the same time inspiring - place and Leeds teams, when backed by the enthusiastic support in the South Stand, invariably play hard, aggressive and skilful rugby. If a visiting team wins there, it has done very well.

Leeds were riding high when Workington visited in the 1978-79 season - they were Challenge cup holders and would go on to finish fourth in the league. Town, on the other hand, had, prior to the game, not been in good form. Earlier in the season the meeting in Cumbria had resulted in a draw for the second consecutive season. A home win seemed the most likely outcome that day at Headingley.

The draw back in September had contained a real tragedy. Peter, injured at the time, watched in horror from the sidelines as John Burke, Workington's expensive signing from Wigan, was injured so badly in a tackle that he had to spend three months recovering in a specialist spinal injuries unit in Hexham near Newcastle before spending a subsequent year in hospital in Southport. After a Workington career which lasted just 16 games, John was confined to a wheelchair, never to play again. Perhaps his appalling injury provided some motivation for the players as they made the lengthy journey to Leeds.

After the tragic injury the Workington players and other individuals rallied round to provide financial support for John and his family. In November 1978, Town challenged their near neighbours Workington Football Club to a charity football game and the rugby players, thanks largely to a skilful display from centre Ian Thompson who scored two goals, gained a very creditable draw. The defence was marshalled by Peter Gorley and the Football Club's forward Peter Foley definitely came off second best on one occasion when he tried to outwit his opponent.

Peter also recalls a sponsored walk in Ennerdale, one of Lakeland's grandest and remotest valleys. There is no road access along either side of the lake there and the walkers, who included Peter, Boxer and some of the lads from Broughton, had to walk round the lake on rough terrain - and, as luck would have it, the weather was the type many visitors associate with Lake District walking - torrential rain. The walk began and ended at the Fox and Hounds pub which was run by West Cumbrian rugby league fan Joe Mather.

On another occasion Peter was part of a minibus party which went to Kendal, to a pub called The Angel which, unfortunately, no longer exists. The landlord, originally from West Cumbria, had placed a large, used whisky bottle on the bar and Peter and his party were entrusted with the task of emptying the bottle, now full of coins, to see how much had been collected for the fund. The people of the Kendal area, not somewhere noted as a hotbed of rugby league, had been very generous.

Cumbrians certainly rallied to the cause and later in another great gesture Les Gorley gave his Great Britain cap to John to keep. John had shown sufficient promise to suggest he himself could have earned one, but fate decreed that he would never find out.

After the 1978 Lancashire Cup Final, Eddie Bowman told Jim Mills how disappointed he was not to have a winner's medal to give to John. Jim knew John from his spell at Workington, and gave his winner's medal to Eddie to give to John. This was a great and kind gesture from one of rugby league's most combative players – and nicest people off the pitch.

Having arrived at Headingley, the Workington players tore up the form book and scattered the pieces to all four corners of Yorkshire's Broad Acres. In the first half the visitors ran away with the game and returned to the dressing room leading 22-5 while the home team was booed off the pitch.

Leeds obviously received a severe half-time lecture from coach Syd Hynes and they came out for the second half with all guns blazing. Peter recalls that at this stage he had to move up to prop after an injury to Harry Beverley. Harry perhaps shouldn't have played because he had collected an eye injury the previous week after an altercation in an international match but as Peter said: "Harry, true to form, didn't let anybody down." However, even Harry, a tough Yorkshire prop, was forced to admit defeat at half time, and Workington reshaped the pack.

The first scrum of the second half broke up in a fracas as fired up Leeds forwards as Graham Joyce, Roy Dickinson and David Ward demonstrated to Peter and Alan Banks that they had a considerable interest in altering the course of the game.

Peter remembers the game's key moment as being not a Workington Town try, but a tackle which rocked its recipient and, indeed, the stadium to its core. Les Dyl, Leeds's international centre, broke through with flying winger John Atkinson in support. He was confronted by Dave 'Shemmy' Collister. If Dyl could deal with the challenge and time his pass correctly, he would surely make another try for his wing colleague to add to his impressive collection. Dyl confidently approached the defender and he was hit by one of the hardest, cruellest, yet fairest tackles that Peter has ever seen in his long career. "That tackle was worth the entrance fee alone," says Peter. Inspired, Workington won 31-11.

Peter played 29 games for Town that season, showing on one occasion in particular that not only was he developing into a top-class second-row forward, but that he also had considerable utility value. In the days when hookers really did hook, he turned out in the hooker's number nine jersey against Featherstone's experienced Ray Handscombe and his contribution helped his team win enough possession to record a very comfortable 29-7 win.

Camaraderie

One fond memory of Peter's of the strong sense of camaraderie between the players and the increasingly large band of supporters was in July 1978 when the Cockermouth branch of the supporters' club organised a competition based on the BBC television show *Superstars* for some entertainment in the close season. Some of the top rugby league names of the day were beaten by a footballer - and a 'Crazy Horse' to boot. However, Emlyn Hughes did have a rugby league background. His father, Fred Hughes, had signed for Barrow in 1936 and 10 years later he moved to Workington where his form was good enough to secure him a place on the 1946 Great Britain tour. Peter did derive some satisfaction by coming out on top that day in the family rivalry stakes.

The final result was:

1. Emlyn Hughes (Liverpool FC) 30 points & a cheque for £150
2. Jimmy Hornby (Wigan) 28 pts
3. Phil Hogan (Barrow) 22 pts
4. Billy Pattinson (W'ton) 21 pts
5. Mal Aspey (Widnes) 20 pts
6. Les Dyl (Leeds) 16 pts
   Steve Nash (Salford) 16 pts
   Eddie Szymala (Barrow) 16 pts
9. Ronnie Fletcher (W'hven) 15 pts
10. Peter Gorley (W'ton) 12 pts
    Harry Beverley (Dewsbury) 12 pts
12. Les Gorley (W'ton) 10 pts
13. Paul Woods (Widnes) 8 pts
14. Phil Cookson (Leeds) 5 pts

Obviously Peter enjoyed playing at Derwent Park far more than most visitors but there were also grounds he particularly enjoyed visiting as a Workington player. He liked Headingley with its consistently good surface, Central Park and Knowsley Road even though he never won there as a visiting player. He didn't enjoy playing at Doncaster's Tattersfield, which he thought was aptly named and he wasn't too impressed with Bramley's McLaren Field which could look bleak and austere in the depths of winter. And once he played at Huyton's tumbledown Alt Park on a wet day where it seemed there was more water on the pitch than there was in the bath afterwards. Again, how times change. None of these grounds is now used for rugby league.

Workington coaches

Peter played under various coaches during his time at Workington. Ike Southward was the coach when the Lancashire Cup was won. He was a Workington legend and only five players have made more appearances for the club. His pedigree as a try scoring winger is beyond question - he scored 274 tries for Workington and a further 100 for Whitehaven and Oldham. He also kicked more than 300 goals during his Derwent Park career and he played 11 times for Great Britain. "He'd done it all," says Peter, "and all the first team got on well with him. He had no airs or graces. He always thought his team had a chance, no matter who we were playing, and this

33

was a big motivational factor." His influence on Peter as an individual and on the team as a whole was unquestionable, particularly on that glorious October day at Warrington.

Peter also thinks that Eric Bell deserves a mention. Eric had been a wonderfully loyal servant to Workington in a career that lasted not far short of 15 years and he appeared more than 200 times as a centre in the 1960s and early 1970s. He was Ike's assistant, and was heavily involved in training sessions. He must take his share of the credit for Town's successes.

Peter also mentions Paul Charlton who, despite being a native of Whitehaven, was Town through and through. A winner, Paul took defeat hard, particularly if it was a home game and the fans at Derwent Park had been disappointed. A complete enthusiast and fitness fanatic who would allegedly run along the beach near his home at St Bees after each game even in the foulest weather Cumbria could produce; he had a very positive attitude which was transmitted to the players in his charge. Paul was, of course, player-coach in 1975-76 on Peter's arrival and he guided the team to promotion, laying the foundations for more success at a higher level.

Peter constantly talks very respectfully of colleagues and opponents alike but he, too, commands great respect. In 2000 he was voted one of the six best Workington players of the 1970s, the others being his brother, Boxer Walker, Eddie Bowman, Ian Wright and Iain MacCorquodale. This great achievement is duly recognised in the players' bar at Derwent Park. He may only have been a Workington player for a relatively short period of time but his influence on the club and its success was clearly enormous.

Boxer recognises Peter's consistent contributions to the team's success. "Peter never let anyone down," said Arnie. "He never had a bad game - he was always good or excellent. Peter will always be a favourite of mine. Whatever medals he has gained, he has deserved. He will go down as a legend in Cumbria. I'm pleased to be a close friend of his."

In action for Workington Town (Photo: *Workington Times & Star*)

35

Tough tackling for Workington Town
(Photo: *Workington Times & Star*)

5. Moving on

They say all good things must come to an end, and such was the case with the accomplishments of the Workington Town team of the late 1970s. The squad which had brought so much success to the club began to break up, and key players left to join Lancashire clubs in pursuit of further honours.

In late 1979 Town reached a fourth successive Lancashire Cup final, but the team which represented the club on that December afternoon at Salford showed wholesale changes in playing personnel: Charlton; MacCorquodale, Maughan, Thompson, Beck; Rudd, Walker; Beverley, Banks, Wallbanks, Pattinson, Lewis, Dobie. Subs: Roper, Varty.

Over half the previous season's final team didn't feature and four powerful forwards - the Gorleys, Eddie Bowman and Bob Blackwood - had left Derwent Park.

This team too was, of course, spurred on by a strong Cumbrian following but spirit and determination were not enough against a talented Widnes team who beat Town again, this time 11-0.

There is no doubt that after Les Gorley's departure for Widnes and Eddie Bowman's transfer to Leigh, fortunes were bound to slump. Peter became disillusioned with life at Derwent Park; he felt, with some apparent justification, that Workington was becoming a selling club, unwilling to invest in the new players needed to maintain the high standards. He trained only once during the summer of 1979 and then made himself unavailable for selection. He asked for a transfer a week after Les's departure for Widnes and his departure became inevitable. Interest in Peter was shown by both Whitehaven and Bradford Northern.

The prospect of moving the few miles down the coast to Whitehaven didn't particularly appeal because Town's local rivals were in the Second Division at that time, but Peter debated long and hard about a move to Odsal. Peter Fox, Bradford's coach, had long been an admirer of the Gorley brothers' talents and Bradford was clearly a team in the ascendancy - it went on to win successive First Division Championships in 1980 and 1981 and the attraction of playing in such a team was obvious. Bradford had missed out on Les and were prepared to pay £25,000 to secure Peter's services, but the stumbling block was their insistence that he move house to live in Yorkshire. Peter enjoyed living in the Cockermouth area where he had been all his life and a move would have been a wrench and hard step to take.

He also took into account his mother's worries. At this time the Yorkshire Ripper was on the loose and Peter Sutcliffe, whose identity was to be revealed a few months later after an extensive police investigation, was brutally murdering women in the city. The streets of Bradford were considered dangerous for young women after dark. Peter managed to set his mum's mind at rest by explaining that strapping rugby forwards were not the Ripper's target and that he could look after himself if he were to relocate to West Yorkshire.

While Peter was mulling over his future, a call came from St Helens, another club who had been impressed by his displays for Workington over the years and they, too, were interested in signing him. By their high standards St Helens had started the season extremely poorly. Widnes had beaten them easily in the first round of the Lancashire Cup at Knowsley Road and two weeks later, again in front of their own fans, Saints were defeated by local rivals Warrington. To make matters worse, they had lost their expensive new signing from Welsh rugby union, goal-kicking full-back Clive Griffiths, with a broken arm. Another defeat five days later at Salford left shocked supporters thumbing the record books to discover when the team had last lost its opening three games in a season.

Clearly team strengthening was necessary and the feeling at Knowsley Road was that Workington's 28-year-old second-rower would fit the bill by providing some much needed forward power. He had acquired plenty of big match experience, arguably he had yet to reach his peak and, all things being equal, he would serve Saints with distinction for a good few seasons to come. History shows the St Helens' board made an excellent choice.

Saints contacted him to say that they would like talks with him one Sunday at Knowsley Road and on the same day Peter, who at this stage was not playing for Workington, took the opportunity to go to watch Town's match away at Widnes. A breakdown in communication resulted in Peter waiting in the bar and then the

38

boardroom at Naughton Park for the arrival of a deputation from St Helens. Surrounded by the Challenge Cup, Regal Trophy and his old friend the Lancashire Cup, Peter perhaps felt that Widnes was really the place to be, but he was waiting for the men from Knowsley Road.

Saints were playing Leeds at Headingley that day but the deputation went first to Widnes by car with the intention of catching the main party later. It was Sunday 7 October 1979 and Peter Gorley became a Saint.

In action for Saints at Widnes August 1980 (Photo: Courtesy Alex Service)

6. Saintly beginnings

So, for the first time since 1971, Workington were left Gorley-less, Peter's departure following that of Les who had departed for Widnes in the summer. The brothers had formed one of Town's best ever second-row pairings, and that is some accolade when it is considered that their positions were once occupied by such greats as Brian Edgar, Norman Herbert and Frank Foster. As Robert Gate wrote in his excellent book *Cumberland Rugby League 100 Greats*, "It was no fun going to Cumberland and being grabbed by the Gorleys, to coin a phrase," and, without being disrespectful to the brothers' successors, visiting forwards were probably relieved they had moved on.

Les, like Peter, was one of the best forwards ever produced in Cumbria, combining strength, size and power with a sleight of hand and an impressive turn of pace for such a big man. He made his Workington debut in March 1971 and went on to play in more than 200 games in his nine year career there, scoring 50 tries, one coming in one of the three Lancashire Cup Finals in which he played such an important role.

His abilities had been noted by other clubs and he signed for Widnes in August 1979, joining one of the game's most powerful teams. He made a winning start in a Lancashire Cup tie at St Helens and over the years became very used to winning, not only matches, but also a host of medals, the first of which came four months into his Widnes career when he collected another Lancashire Cup winners' medal. It was a touch ironic that his new club beat the club he had left that summer.

Three winners' medals in the Premiership followed and Les also achieved the ambition of every player when he appeared at Wembley - three times, in fact. And he was undefeated at the famous old stadium, although after the drawn final in 1982, Widnes did lose to Hull in the replay at Elland Road in Leeds.

Playing for a bigger club with higher profile players helped Les gain to international recognition. He appeared five times for Great Britain between 1980 and 1982, but with only limited success. He was sent off playing for his country in a stormy game in France and his international career, like that of some other players, was brought to a close when the amazing, all-conquering 1982 Australian tourists highlighted immense shortcomings in the British game. Les was also capped twice for England once, in 1977, while still at Workington, suggesting that the selectors did occasionally look north to the game's outposts.

As one of Cumbria's finest it was obvious he would receive the call to represent his county and he did so 16 times in eight years beginning in 1973, rating his role in Cumbria's championship-winning team as one of his favourite memories.

Les's last game for Widnes was in 1984 when he helped the Chemics defeat Wigan at Wembley and in November that year he moved on to finish his career at Whitehaven.

Peter followed big brother's example and took the southbound M6 in search of fame, fortune and success. Les had acclimatised well to his new club in South Lancashire - would Peter to do the same?

He did not have to wait long for his Saints debut. St Helens at this time was a club in turmoil and Peter had not been signed as a promising youngster who would have to play in the 'A' team and patiently wait for his chance to hit the big time; rather, he was a recognised star player who had come on something of a rescue mission. His presence would add steel and fire to the pack, and there was no time to lose in ensuring that he quickly became an integral part of the Saints set up if the season was to be saved.

Two days after signing, Peter made his first appearance in the famous red and white strip, despite the fact that, on his own admission, he was not match fit. However, his overall fitness level had always been high - it must have been, because he missed very few matches in his Workington Town career. He went straight into the first team to provide a fresh face, more power to the forwards and some interest for the fans who were rapidly becoming very disillusioned with what they had been seeing.

The occasion was a home tie in the now defunct BBC2 Floodlit Trophy competition against Rochdale Hornets. The visitors at that time were an average Second Division side and perhaps did not present as great a challenge as some of the First Division big guns would have done, but nevertheless the nerves were certainly jangling as Peter made his way down from Cumbria to Lancashire.

Peter would often look for company on the long trip down the M6 and on this occasion he travelled down with his former colleague Dave Collister (of 'Headingley tackle' fame). He recalls going into the dressing room and recognising so many of his team-mates either because he had played against them during his time at Workington, or because he had seen them in high profile matches on television. This was the turning point of his career - "This is where my career really takes off," thought Peter, as he sat down in the company of his new colleagues.

The Saints fans warmed to their new Cumbrian hero as Peter enjoyed a great debut. As predicted, Saints won quite easily and Peter played a starring role, setting up two early tries to send Saints on their way. Near the end came the icing on the cake as Peter took a pass from Harry Pinner, a superb player destined to become Peter's best friend at St Helens, and crashed over for the first of the 46 tries he would score for his new club. St Helens beat Rochdale 45-17 after leading 15-9 at half time.

St Helens: Parkes; Litherland, Glynn, Haggerty, Mathias; Peters, K. Gwilliam; James, Liptrot, E. Chisnall, Nicholls, Gorley, Pinner. Subs: Smith, Seldon.

Rochdale Hornets: Bailey; Holland, McGiffen, Houghton, Marsh; Gilmore, Sanderson; Wilson, Langan, Smith, Grimes, Duffy, Doherty. Subs: Rawlinson, Coates.

Saints' tries came from Peters and Mathias, who both scored two, plus Glynn, Haggerty, Gwilliam, Gorley and Pinner, who also kicked nine goals. Rochdale's tries were scored by Holland, Marsh, Grimes and Rawlinson. Wilson added two goals and a drop goal; and Peter's debut was refereed by Mr Smith of Halifax.

Peter's first return journey north was a pleasant one - it had been a job well done. As the St Helens supporters in the crowd that night wended their way home they began to wonder whether the latest acquisition from the Cumbrian coast would prove to be as successful as players such as Dick Huddart and John Tembey who, in the past, had made similar journeys, albeit from Workington's rivals Whitehaven. Only time would tell, but the signs were promising.

The teams from the programme for Peter's debut for St Helens)

(Courtesy St Helens RLFC)

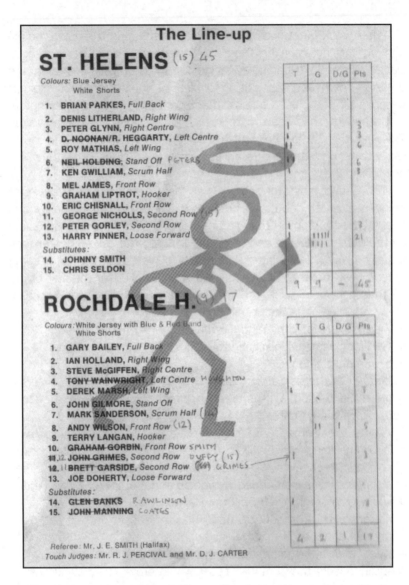

The Line-up

ST. HELENS (15) 45

Colours: Blue Jersey
White Shorts

		T	G	D/G	Pts
1.	BRIAN PARKES, *Full Back*				
2.	DENIS LITHERLAND, *Right Wing*				
3.	PETER GLYNN, *Right Centre*	1			3
4.	~~D. NOONAN~~/R. HEGGARTY, *Left Centre*	1			3
5.	ROY MATHIAS, *Left Wing*	11			6
6.	~~NEIL HOLDING~~, *Stand Off* PETERS	11			6
7.	KEN GWILLIAM, *Scrum Half*				3
8.	MEL JAMES, *Front Row*				
9.	GRAHAM LIPTROT, *Hooker*				
10.	ERIC CHISNALL, *Front Row*				
11.	GEORGE NICHOLLS, *Second Row* (15)				
12.	PETER GORLEY, *Second Row*	1			3
13.	HARRY PINNER, *Loose Forward*		11111 11111		21
Substitutes:					
14.	JOHNNY SMITH				
15.	CHRIS SELDON				
		9	9	-	45

ROCHDALE H. (9) 7

Colours: White Jersey with Blue & Red Band
White Shorts

		T	G	D/G	Pts
1.	GARY BAILEY, *Full Back*	1			3
2.	IAN HOLLAND, *Right Wing*				
3.	STEVE McGIFFEN, *Right Centre*				
4.	~~TONY WAINWRIGHT~~, *Left Centre* HOUGHTON				
5.	DEREK MARSH, *Left Wing*	1			3
6.	JOHN GILMORE, *Stand Off*				
7.	MARK SANDERSON, *Scrum Half*				
8.	ANDY WILSON, *Front Row* (12)		11	1	5
9.	TERRY LANGAN, *Hooker*				
10.	~~GRAHAM GORBIN~~, *Front Row* SMITH				
~~11.~~ 12.	JOHN GRIMES, *Second Row* DUFFY (15)	1			3
12. 11	BRETT GARSIDE, *Second Row* GRIMES				
13.	JOE DOHERTY, *Loose Forward*				
Substitutes:					
14.	~~GLEN BANKS~~ RAWLINSON	1			3
15.	~~JOHN MANNING~~ COATES				
		4	3	1	17

Referee: Mr. J. E. SMITH (Halifax)
Touch Judges: Mr. R. J. PERCIVAL and Mr. D. J. CARTER

On the following Sunday Saints were at home again, this time against stronger opposition, reigning Champions Hull Kingston Rovers. Despite victories in the Floodlit Trophy against Oldham and Rochdale and a John Player success at Barrow, St Helens had yet to record a win in the League. It was mid-October, the team had not

44

defeated First Division opposition and, although the visiting supporters humorously informed everyone of the 'pointlessness' of Saints' situation, the players were as aware of this as anybody and didn't need any reminders. The big guns from Hull must have really fancied their chances of recording a rare win at Knowsley Road.

On the cover of the match programme was a picture of "The mighty Cumbrian Peter Gorley who delighted Saints fans with his outstanding display on Tuesday". He had already made an impression. The teams for his St Helens league debut were:

St Helens: Parkes; Litherland, Glynn, Peters, Mathias; Holding, K. Gwilliam; James, Liptrot, E. Chisnall, Seldon, Gorley, Pinner. Subs: Haggerty, D. Chisnall

Hull KR: Leighton; Hubbard, Smith, Watson, Sullivan; Hartley, Agar; Holdstock, Heslop, Millington, Lowe, Madley, Hall.
Subs: Harkin, Crookes

On paper the visitors looked too strong for the home side but Saints, perhaps inspired by the latest big-money signing which promised better times to come, produced their best performance of the season. Thanks to a wonderful winger's try by Denis Litherland and other tries by fellow threequarters Peter Glynn and Steve Peters, plus three goals from Harry Pinner, St Helens were able to turn a 5-0 deficit into a 15-7 victory. For the record, the visitors' points came courtesy of a try by Clive Sullivan, whose son Anthony later became a Saints hero, and two goals from Steve Hubbard.

Unfortunately, the proceedings were to end in tragic circumstances when the referee, Joe Jackson, collapsed and died after the match. It was one of those occurrences which really did serve to put sport into perspective. Notwithstanding this terrible tragedy, Peter's first league game at Knowsley Road had been successful for him and the team. Having opened their season's account in the best possible way, Saints would surely now go on to provide the fans with more thrilling moments.

Playing for St Helens against Bradford Northern at Knowsley Road
(Photo: Courtesy Alex Service)

7. Settling in fast

It may have been coincidence - but then again, maybe not - that Peter's arrival marked the start of a lengthy unbeaten run for St Helens, as the team embarked on a sequence of seven games undefeated, five of which were at home, giving the newest Saint plenty of opportunity to become accustomed to his new surroundings. He quickly made one of the second-row positions his own and settled down readily, instantly providing the pack with much needed strength and mobility and winning the man-of-the-match award against Blackpool. It was not until the end of November that Peter collected losing pay when Saints lost at Odsal in a match specially rearranged to mark the first use of Bradford Northern's new floodlights.

One match which stood out on the fixture list was played two days before Christmas when Workington were set to visit Knowsley Road. Peter must have had mixed feelings that Sunday teatime after his new team had thrashed his old team 51-0. Ruthless in both halves, Saints recorded 11 tries, five of which came from Welsh winger Roy Mathias as he equalled his own record of tries in a First Division match which he had already set in a match against Rochdale in the first season of two-division rugby. The result justified Peter's move to Lancashire and suggested that he had a much better chance of enjoying success in his new surroundings although Workington recovered from the thrashing sufficiently well to survive in the First Division that season, and towards the end of the campaign they beat Saints quite comfortably at Derwent Park.

Three days later Peter found himself enjoying the special atmosphere of a Saints versus Wigan derby match for the first time. Wigan were not enjoying a successful period, and were struggling near the bottom of the table. Saints' support then did not compare favourably with that which they enjoy in the Super League era, and so a disappointing attendance of 7,263 gathered at Central Park on Boxing Day to see the visitors win 16-10 thanks largely to a hat-trick of tries by Harry Pinner – who became the only St Helens forward to perform this feat in a derby match. The return match in April 1980 saw Peter register his first try against Wigan - the first of five he was to score in total against the old enemy - as Saints won 20-17 to complete the double and help exile Wigan to the Second Division for a season. Peter became a bit of a talisman for Saints in these early local clashes because he was on the winning side in his first three derbies and when he missed two out of the three derbies in the 1981-82 season, Saints lost. He went on to play in 15 such games, being victorious eight times.

Workington were back at Knowsley Road soon after the new year in the first round of the Challenge Cup and although, according to the match programme, Peter wasn't originally selected to play, he did take his place in the familiar number 12 jersey. As was the case before Christmas, the Cumbrians headed home defeated but the result was a far more respectable 16-0. Peter's first Wembley campaign as a Saint was underway although it didn't last much longer, eventual League champions Bradford winning a very close game 11-10 at Knowsley Road in the second round. Sadly, Peter was never to reach the Holy Grail of a Wembley Final.

Probably more important for Peter than matches against Wigan or Workington were the fixtures against Widnes which allowed him to lock horns with his brother. Traditionally arranged for New Year's Day and Easter Monday, the first match fell victim to the weather, and both games took place within six days of each other in April. Widnes, together with Bradford, were chasing the Championship title, and St Helens gave their credentials a stiff examination on Easter Monday in losing 16-9 at Naughton Park, but six days later a much weakened Saints team lost the return match 19-0. Les triumphed in the fraternal battle - and not for the last time - but Peter would certainly have his moments when they met up again.

Peter's first season saw Saints finish in eighth place and, in truth, a long way from honours; the team was in something of a transition phase but Peter was greatly enjoying his time at Knowsley Road, building his reputation as a highly capable forward who would go on to more glorious times as a stronger Saints squad began to take shape.

8. 1980-81: Saints build a future

Peter's first full season as a Saint began in mid-August 1980 and the luck of the draw in the Lancashire Cup took him back home to Derwent Park to face old friends which, of course, rekindled memories of previous successful early season cup campaigns. As mentioned before, Workington had been beaten finalists the previous year and no doubt fancied a fifth consecutive final, but St Helens had other ideas and a crowd of nearly 3,000 saw the visitors win 15-5. Town's love affair with the competition was over, and they never did reach another final, while Saints unluckily went no further than the following week when, despite matching Widnes try-for-try - one of them by Peter - two Keith Elwell drop-goals were decisive in a narrow 22-20 defeat at Naughton Park.

The start of the league campaign produced a real challenge as Bradford Northern, reigning League Champions, stormed into town. Bradford had beaten Saints four times the previous season and were doubtless confident of further success, but Saints turned the tables in style with a convincing 16-6 victory, scoring four tries while keeping their own line intact. It was looking highly promising, but inconsistency soon set in and some disappointments were to follow.

The pattern of the season developed as: win some, lose some; and it wasn't long before Peter had to handle the first disappointment of his Saints career, falling to an injury jinx which seemed to haunt Knowsley Road. Having scored an important try in a home game against Featherstone Rovers which helped to secure a vital win for his side, he was forced off with a serious ankle injury which kept him out for the next six weeks. The injury probably cost him two appearances against the touring New Zealanders - one for Saints and one for Cumbria, for his form would surely have merited county selection. In his absence only one St Helens game, the one against the Kiwis, was won.

Peter gave a great display on his return to the team in a win at Leigh, and he was back in the groove for Workington's visit the following week. Town had found it difficult to replace their departing stars and were struggling at the foot of the table with only one league victory - against Halifax the previous week - to show for their efforts. Indeed, at the end of the season they were to be relegated, so it was no big surprise when Saints won 18-8. There was some consolation in defeat for Alan Varty, Peter's great friend from Broughton, who scored both his team's tries that day.

From a position to make perhaps an audacious bid for league glory after beating Workington in the middle of November, Saints hit a disastrous patch winning only four of the next 13 games, including losing in the first round of the John Player Trophy at home to Warrington. The team did not win again after the Workington match before Boxing Day when, on a grey and dismal afternoon, a last-minute try from Mick Hope was needed to secure victory over Oldham. Saints' second lowest crowd of the season, 4,136, saw the victory - a far cry from former times when the ground would have been full for Wigan's holiday season visit.

Wigan, of course, were otherwise engaged, losing a Second Division match at the late, lamented Station Road, Swinton - now a housing estate. The crowd there wasn't much smaller than that at the Saints game. At the end of the season, Saints' old rivals were promoted, however, as runners-up to York and arguably rugby league's greatest derby fixture was able to resume the next season.

As the Saints team began to emerge from the depths of winter in mid-February, the Challenge Cup was the last trophy for which it could realistically aim. And, it reached the semi-final with a great economy of scoring, needing a mere 21 points in total to beat Huddersfield, Hull and Oldham - a statistic which modern day fans of 21st century rugby league would find very difficult to believe. Never was the winning margin greater than two points - heavy going for both supporters and players, particularly those of a nervous disposition.

The second round victory against Hull, finalists the previous year, was the most creditable. Saints fans' abiding memory of that Saturday is arriving in good time at their normal place on the Popular Side to find it was a sea of black and white. It had been completely taken over by the visitors from the east coast. There wasn't a home supporter in sight so they retreated to the Paddock. Such terrace drama has never been witnessed before or since. However, the

Saints fans huddled together had the last laugh, as they saw Peter Glynn score the crucial try under the posts at the clubhouse end in the first half. Even another unfortunate injury to Peter Gorley couldn't stop Saints' progress. Was a Wembley Final beckoning?

Semi-final

By the time the semi-final on 4 April arrived there was a belief in the town that a spring visit to Wembley was once more in the offing and Saints were well represented in the 17,000 crowd which gathered at Headingley to see the clash with Hull Kingston Rovers. The Hull side were higher in the table and generally expected to win, but Saints had done the double over them in the league and they knew they were in with a good chance. For a long time there was little to choose between the teams but a late burst of scoring gave Hull KR a rather flattering 22-5 win, Harry Pinner's try and Clive Griffiths's goal being Saints' only consolation. As well as many disappointed Saints supporters that day there was a disappointed Widnes forward. Saints' neighbours had qualified for the final the week before and Les Gorley was rooting for St Helens, for obvious reasons. However, the brotherly showdown on the hallowed Wembley turf was not set to materialise.

Starting with the cup trip to Huddersfield, Saints embarked on a run of 10 wins in 14 matches to finish the season with a flourish and the team's improved efforts were mirrored by Peter who scored six tries in the last seven matches. The sequence included an impressive Easter Sunday win against Hull which featured Peter's only two-try scoring feat for the club and a victorious trip to champions Bradford in the Premiership play-offs. However, Hull Kingston Rovers ended Saints' interest in the Premiership with a 30-17 semi-final victory. Peter scored one of Saints' tries.

All in all, as the season concluded in May there was justifiable optimism. Peter's efforts - nine tries in 31 matches - were a key reason behind the optimism and he had become an indispensable part of the Saints set up.

Supporting Harry Pinner playing for St Helens at Knowsley Road
(Photo: Courtesy Alex Service)

9. 1981-82: Autumn optimism

Optimism was rife in rugby league during the late summer and early autumn of 1981. Expansion was the name of the game.

London's new outpost club, Fulham, were looking forward to top flight rugby league having gained promotion in its first season. In 1980-81 the team had consisted of good, experienced professionals such as Harry Beverley, John Risman and Iain MacCorquodale all of whom, of course, had played with Peter at Workington, and they all played key roles, particularly Corky who was still able to kick goals from anywhere. However, Risman and MacCorquodale did not feature with Fulham in the First Division; having helped the club to promotion they signed for Blackpool together with giant forward Ian van Bellen, another hero of Fulham's first season.

Suitably inspired, new teams were formed in Cardiff and Carlisle and they looked forward to emulating Fulham's feat. Both looked strong, featuring, like Fulham, experienced players with Cardiff having a strong St Helens flavour. Among their players were three of Peter's team mates from his Saints debut - George Nicholls, Ken Gwilliam and Chris Seldon - plus hooker Denis Nulty.

Meanwhile, optimism at Knowsley Road was based on the conclusion to the previous season. Were things about to move in the right direction?

In the summer of 1981 the St Helens team trained hard under coach Kel Coslett and when the season started in mid-August, the players were ready. The new campaign began with the Lancashire Cup and Saints started like a house on fire winning 28-0 at Blackpool and then crushing Barrow at home. Barrow were confident: they had knocked out holders Warrington in the first round, but they were no match for the Saints. Peter enjoyed a reunion with Howard Allen, now Barrow's hooker, and they exchanged tries in Saints' 40-17 win.

The league programme began with a visit from Fulham, keen to prove their worth against the big boys. But the Londoners found Saints a different proposition from their opponents the previous season and just short of 6,000 fans saw them beaten 35-4. They were particularly undone by the other Peter G in Saints' colours - Peter Glynn, who, playing full-back, scored 26 points with four tries and seven goals and was close to the club record for points in a match. After three matches Saints had rattled up 103 points and Peter Gorley had scored in each game.

However, Saints progressed no further in the Lancashire Cup, losing 20-6 to eventual winners Leigh at Hilton Park, but then they put paid to the unbeaten starts of both Castleford (with Peter scoring again) and Leigh, further suggesting that they were a team going places. They did not, though, receive the recognition they deserved from the press - or at least some fans didn't think they did, as the following letter I had published in the *Rugby Leaguer* under the heading "Convincing enough for me!" on 15 October suggested: "So Don Yates thinks Saints have not been 'too convincing' so far this season. Perhaps he hasn't noticed the 40 points against Barrow, 35 against Fulham, 33 against Wakefield and 32 at Castleford. Also they are the only team to beat Leigh this season. He must be very hard to please!"

In October the John Player Trophy - another competition that no longer exists - began. Saints were drawn to play Barrow at Knowsley Road. With memories of the Lancashire Cup tie fresh in their minds Saints were favourites to progress, but the Furnessmen had indulged in a little shrewd team strengthening. They were a fair side in those days and had a trick or two up their sleeves. They outscored the home team four tries to three and went back north with a very satisfying 16-16 draw. Yet, as was becoming commonplace, the name Gorley featured on the St Helens scoresheet.

This try had particular significance because it led to Peter's appearance in the RFL's list of top ten try scorers - a justifiable source of great satisfaction to him. He had now scored six tries for his club and one for his county and so the list on October 22 read:

Steve Hartley (Hull KR)	11	Green Vigo (Swinton)	8
John Jones (Workington T)	11	John Woods (Leigh)	8
John Buckton (Doncaster)	10	Keith Bentley (Widnes)	7
Des Drummond (Leigh)	10	Peter Glynn (St Helens)	7
John Basnett (Widnes)	8	Peter Gorley (St Helens)	7
Chris Harrison (Hull)	8	Stuart Wright (Widnes)	7

Peter is the only forward on that list which is some achievement. Unfortunately, the pleasure derived from reading this list was tainted later that evening. A journey up to Barrow - or, in Peter's case, a trip down the Cumbrian coast - was needed for the replayed cup tie and, if Barrow could reproduce the previous Sunday's form, a tough match was in prospect. Nevertheless, Saints took to the M6 in confident mood. The subsequent 17-0 defeat was hugely disappointing and had apparent repercussions.

Form became sketchy, but this wasn't helped by a long exile from Knowsley Road as three consecutive home games were postponed for various reasons. Keen to strengthen the pack and to add to Peter's forceful second-row play, the club signed Gary Moorby, a hard-running player with a reputation for try scoring, from Keighley. He began well with a try and winning pay on his debut at Bradford, Peter moving to loose-forward that day to accommodate him.

Saints spent an amazing two and a half months on the road and after the Barrow trophy upset collected five points from as many league games - fair, but hardly championship form. Peter's tries dried up and he missed the reunion with former Workington team mate Boxer Walker at Whitehaven's Recreation Ground before the severe winter weather arrived.

The next time Saints fans saw their heroes was New Year's Day. However, 'saw' is used loosely here because Knowsley Road was enveloped in thick fog. Referee Stan Wall stood at the centre of the two 25-yard lines and was able to see the corner flags and therefore, according to the rules, visibility was good enough for the match to be played. The star-studded Widnes team rode into Knowsley Road but supporters who weren't standing around the half-way line would have needed radar to locate the players. Through the gloom they could just about make out the Gorley brothers in direct competition and this and other interesting individual contests came into view and then disappeared again from time to time. From a spectator's point of view, the match should not have started but Peter was not complaining; he was back on the try trail and Saints won 13-10.

Then the wheels fell off. A dreadful run of six defeats in seven games included a catastrophic home loss to Castleford, when 40 points were conceded. The programme notes for the York match at the end of January - the only win in that disastrous sequence - summed the situation up well: "Everyone connected with the club is concerned with the size and manner of the recent defeats, not least the players themselves. They are playing with a complete lack of confidence that is obvious to anyone... You can be sure of one thing - that confidence will diminish even further without the support of our own fans."

Fewer than 3,000 supporters read those words. Knowsley Road was not a happy place. By this stage Peter was sidelined, having been injured in a defeat at Leigh and he was absent for arguably the greatest disappointment of the season - a home loss to Wigan in the first round of the Challenge Cup. In a terrible run of form, optimism for a trip to Wembley was not great, but Wigan had a mediocre team and Saints would have fancied their chances of making progress. It had been 13 years since Saints had suffered a first round Challenge Cup knockout when, in 1968, they lost 5-0 to Huddersfield on a quagmire at Knowsley Road, but history counted for nothing. The visitors, inspired by David Stephenson who had a great game on his debut after a big money transfer from Salford, won quite comfortably 20-12 but made no further progress themselves, losing at Central Park to Widnes in the second round.

Peter returned the following week at York as something of a salvage operation began and, with the Cumbrian back in the side, St Helens won eight of the next nine matches. Was this coincidence?

He was back on the try trail the week before Easter even though Saints lost at home to a powerful Hull Kingston Rovers team and on Good Friday he scored a crucial try as this time Wigan were beaten at Knowsley Road. This was followed up by a brilliant win on Easter Monday at Widnes which made supporters wonder if an unlikely tilt at the Premiership was on the cards. Alas, a trip to Hull with a weakened side proved to be a task that was too demanding.

Saints seemed to have made little progress but Peter had personally enjoyed a good season. Despite his injury, only Roy Haggerty, John Butler (a St Helens local acquired from Wigan at the start of the season), Peter Glynn and Chris Arkwright had played more games, and only Haggerty and Arkwright scored more than Peter's 11 tries. Peter won the supporters' club player-of-the-season award. As in the summer of 1981, there was a feeling that better times were round the corner.

But how did rugby league's new kids on the block fare? Fulham finished their season fourth from the bottom of the table and unfortunately suffered relegation, although they did record a great win over eventual champions Leigh. Carlisle, inspired by Trumanns Man of Steel winner Mick Morgan, their try scoring prop forward, won 28 games out of 32 to finish runners up to Oldham in the Second Division, but Cardiff, after a promising start - almost 10,000 fans attended the first match against Salford - fell away alarmingly, and finished eighth in the Second Division.

Going forward for St Helens
(Photo: Courtesy Alex Service)

10. 1982-3: Finally a St Helens final

The following season began with a new coach at Knowsley Road. After nearly two years at the helm, Kel Coslett parted company with St Helens. Alex Murphy was tipped to make the short journey from Leigh to take over, but instead he was tempted to Central Park in an attempt to initiate rivals Wigan's renaissance and Billy Benyon was appointed St Helens coach.

Billy is a St Helens legend. Locally born, he turned down the chance to play football with Bolton Wanderers in order to sign for Saints, and he became one of only four players to make more than 500 first team appearances. He played in 20 major finals, featuring in three victorious Wembley teams. His 15-year career was littered with honours before he departed for Warrington where he arrived just in time to collect a John Player Trophy winners' medal to complete his collection. He coached Warrington for nearly four years during which time Warrington won the John Player Trophy again, in 1981. He lost his job at Wilderspool in March 1982, despite having been Trumanns Coach of the Year in 1981. The players felt the sacking was extremely unjust and two of them, forwards Brian Case and Neil Courtney, submitted transfer requests in protest.

So Benyon came with a good pedigree. His likeable manner and impressive methods soon won him the respect of Peter, who responded well to him.

Billy Benyon had a high regard for Peter: "Having played against Peter on several occasions in my career I knew that he was a model professional. On my return to St Helens as coach Peter was already part the squad and I always had a great respect for him. He travelled from Cumbria for training sessions and rarely missed one. Players were proud to play with him and he always gave his all on the field. He was part of a wonderful team which contributed to my successful time at the club."

The opening fixtures were not easy. St Helens had been sent to Leigh for the first match of the new season. The championship trophy was sitting proudly in the Hilton Park boardroom and their players were out to impress Colin Clarke, the new Leigh coach, so Saints, trailing at half time, did well to share the spoils in a 19-19 draw. The point was secured when a last-minute try in the corner by young forward Gary Bottell was brilliantly converted by Neil Holding. "Peter Gorley had a super game and how the Great Britain selectors can continue to overlook him is something of a mystery," was written in the programme for Saints' first home game on the following Wednesday when Peter followed up his try at Leigh with another one against Bradford.

An arm injury meant Peter missed the trip to Hull Kingston Rovers to help Rovers celebrate 60 years of rugby at Craven Park and the following Friday he found himself under the surgeon's knife at Whiston Hospital. It seemed he was set to miss the Lancashire Cup tie at Widnes on the Sunday.

A piece of floating bone was removed from his elbow and, safely stitched up, Peter drove back to Cumbria. The elbow stitches were still secure when he arrived home.

On the Sunday he travelled to Widnes with his brother and he recalls sitting in the dressing room next to hooker Graham Liptrot who was set to play his first match after recovering from a fractured jaw. Graham was impressed by Peter having travelled such a distance just to support the team. "I've not come to watch, I've come to play," was the amazing reply. "The stitches can be wrapped up, so I'll be OK." Graham, himself a tough lad who had to recover from more than one broken jaw, could scarcely believe it.

Peter didn't just play - he played a key role. After trailing at half time, Saints fought back with a try from full-back and man-of-the-match John Butler but then Widnes introduced star substitute Andy Gregory who was returning after a minor knee operation. His arrival did the trick and he scooted over for a try to put the home team back in front. It wasn't to last; Peter recalls that with about 10 minutes to go he took a pass from Roy Haggerty and scored the winning try which Neil Holding coolly converted.

Later he discovered the stitches had been dislodged, and the other players could scarcely believe the extent of the injury. "But I felt no pain," said Peter. "It was such a great feeling to have scored the winning try - some revenge for those Lancashire Cup Final defeats against Widnes." This match represents one of Peter's fondest - and, despite what he says, probably most painful - memories of his time at Knowsley Road.

Widnes: Lydon; Wright, O'Loughlin, Burke, Basnett; Hughes, Hulme; M. O'Neill, Elwell, S. O'Neill, L. Gorley, Prescott, Adams. Subs: Gregory, Whitfield.

St Helens: Butler; Meadows, Glynn, Haggerty, Litherland; Holding, Peters; Owen, Liptrot, Bottell, Moorby, P. Gorley, Pinner. Subs: Parkes, Mathias.

Gorley sets up Saints stunner

One of the headlines from the Widnes match

Stand-off Neil Holding kicked four goals to add to the tries. For Widnes, Mick Adams also scored a try - there was no controversy surrounding Stuart Wright this time - and Mick Burke kicked three goals. A crowd of 6,704 people saw it all - except, of course, for the sight of Gorley's gory arm afterwards.

During his time at Workington Peter had played on occasions when perhaps he shouldn't have done owing to injury. Of course, his team-mates did too because the squad was quite small. "This injury wasn't serious," he thought, "so why not play now?"

The next match in the Lancashire Cup was at Barrow but this time the Craven Park cup obstacle was overcome, Saints just winning 9-6. Saints then returned to Barrow for a second time four days later in a league match when Barrow gained revenge. Guess which match Peter missed?

The cup win took Saints to the semi-final stage and a home tie with Carlisle who had knocked out holders Leigh sensationally in the previous round. Although they were a fellow First Division side, no one really expected them to give much trouble, despite their Hilton Park heroics.

Saints were lucky to escape with a 7-7 draw, many spectators believing the visitors deserved to win. A tough looking trip north the

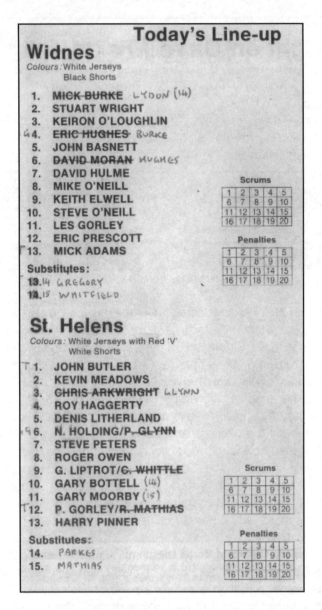

Today's Line-up

Widnes

Colours: White Jerseys
Black Shorts

1. ~~MICK BURKE~~ LYDON (14)
2. STUART WRIGHT
3. KEIRON O'LOUGHLIN
4. ~~ERIC HUGHES~~ BURKE
5. JOHN BASNETT
6. ~~DAVID MORAN~~ HUGHES
7. DAVID HULME
8. MIKE O'NEILL
9. KEITH ELWELL
10. STEVE O'NEILL
11. LES GORLEY
12. ERIC PRESCOTT
13. MICK ADAMS

Substitutes:

~~13.~~ 14 GREGORY
~~14.~~ 15 WHITFIELD

Scrums

1	2	3	4	5
6	7	8	9	10
11	12	13	14	15
16	17	18	19	20

Penalties

1	2	3	4	5
6	7	8	9	10
11	12	13	14	15
16	17	18	19	20

St. Helens

Colours: White Jerseys with Red 'V'
White Shorts

1. JOHN BUTLER
2. KEVIN MEADOWS
3. ~~CHRIS ARKWRIGHT~~ GLYNN
4. ROY HAGGERTY
5. DENIS LITHERLAND
6. N. HOLDING/~~P. GLYNN~~
7. STEVE PETERS
8. ROGER OWEN
9. G. LIPTROT/~~G. WHITTLE~~
10. GARY BOTTELL (14)
11. GARY MOORBY (15)
12. P. GORLEY/~~R. MATHIAS~~
13. HARRY PINNER

Substitutes:

14. PARKES
15. MATHIAS

Scrums

1	2	3	4	5
6	7	8	9	10
11	12	13	14	15
16	17	18	19	20

Penalties

1	2	3	4	5
6	7	8	9	10
11	12	13	14	15
16	17	18	19	20

The teams from the Widnes versus St Helens match, with the Gorley brothers on opposing sides (Courtesy Widnes Vikings RLFC) following Wednesday for the replay was not quite what the doctor had ordered. Peter set off from his West Cumbrian home to meet his team-mates fully expecting a challenging evening. Ironically, he was the only Cumbrian on the pitch.

Challenging it certainly was but, greatly helped by Peter's man-of-the-match performance and Graham Liptrot's first half scrum monopolisation, St Helens won the match 9-5. Denis Litherland was the try scorer that night and drop-goal king Harry Pinner contributed three successful efforts. In a hard game, Chris Arkwright and Dean Bell were sent off after a flare-up.

At last Peter had enjoyed a significant cup run in St Helens colours and Warrington were to be the opposition at Wigan's Central Park in the final.

Before that there was the matter of a tour match with the Australians at Knowsley Road. As a club, St Helens' record against the Kangaroos was as good as anybody's but the match was less than a week before the final and, fearful of injuries, it was decided some key personnel, Peter included, should miss the game. In a hopeless mismatch the Australians, themselves clearly not operating at full throttle despite selecting their test team, won easily 32-0. Saints' supporters marvelled at the skill level of players like Mal Meninga, not realising at that stage how much he would thrill them in a couple of years, but they left feeling cheated and hardly in the best of spirits for the following week.

Lancashire Cup Final

And things didn't improve as the Saints fans endured a miserable Saturday afternoon in Wigan. The first disappointment was the attendance figure - fewer than 6,500 for a local derby final was a poor turnout, but Saints' performance was a bigger disappointment, especially given the fact that their better players had returned. Although the first half was close, Warrington romped away after the break and they took the cup 16-0.

Warrington's key player was ace marksman Steve Hesford who was voted man-of-the-match, ironically despite missing no fewer than seven attempts at goal. It was Hesford who created the only try of the first half when he caught his own kick and sent in Paul Fellows at the corner while shortly after half-time he seized on a kick by Bob Eccles to put Mike Kelly in at the other corner. His touchline conversion signalled the end of the St Helens challenge and when Graham Liptrot, who had been winning the scrums by a 3:1 ratio was sent off after a foul on Carl Webb, the game was up. Eccles - for the sixth consecutive match - and Wire's captain and former Saint Ken Kelly scored further tries to make it even worse.

St Helens: Parkes; Ledger, Arkwright, Haggerty, Litherland; Peters, Holding; James, Liptrot, Bottell, Moorby, Gorley, Pinner.
Subs: Smith, Mathias.

Warrington: Hesford; Fellows, R. Duane, Bevan, M. Kelly; Cullen, K. Kelly; Courtney, Webb, Cooke, Fieldhouse, Eccles, M. Gregory.
Subs; Finnegan, D. Chisnall.

It is interesting to note that, in 2004 at the start of Super League IX, two of the Warrington team - Paul Cullen and Mike Gregory – are now Super League coaches.

Peter's first final in Saints colours had gone badly wrong and the season clearly needed rescuing. Yet this time the repercussions did not seem as serious as those after the cup defeat at Barrow the previous year and, despite the Central Park disaster, grounds for optimism were still apparent.

Immediately after the final a new Saint was greeted as giant forward Paul Grimes signed from Whitehaven. He made his debut the following week in the league against Warrington when Saints, perhaps rather infuriatingly, won. 'Jethro', as he was known on the Knowsley Road Popular Side, became a crowd favourite, stiffened up the pack and gave the club very good service for a couple of seasons. Another plus was the emergence of Barry Ledger who was in his first full season as a first-teamer. In one spell he scored in eight games out of nine and showed great promise as a speedy winger and a strong finisher.

Peter again hit the headlines in mid-November when Saints visited Workington. He had missed Town's visit to Knowsley Road in September but this time he featured prominently as the headline confirmed: "Gorley goes home to prove a point." The report began: "Prime Cumbrian export Peter Gorley went home to Workington on

Sunday to prove a point to his old followers - and perhaps to the Great Britain selectors." There was a definite groundswell of opinion at the time that believed he deserved an international recall.

On a foul day, with standing water on the pitch, the teams produced a far better game than anyone had a right to expect and although Workington had not won since mid-September, they held a 10-7 lead at half time before a blast of two tries in three minutes helped Saints to a 20-15 win and their first league double of the season. Town's poor run of form and the Cumbrian weather led to a crowd of only 995 people. Where were all the supporters from the Lancashire Cup years?

There were upsets along the way - a John Player Trophy defeat to a Graeme West-inspired Wigan was hard to take, but things seemed to be moving in the right direction. Certainly revenge was sweet on Boxing Day when Peter's try helped defeat Wigan at Knowsley Road. It came at a crucial time because there was little to choose between the two teams before Peter scored with 14 minutes remaining to tip the balance.

The new year of 1983 began well both for the team, which extended its successful sequence after the Wigan trophy defeat to 10 wins in 11 games, and for Peter who was appointed team captain in the absence through injury of Harry Pinner.

Peter did, however, notch up an unwanted 'first'. On 1 January 1983 the sin bin was introduced into British rugby league and Peter was the first Saint to sit in it, at Wheldon Road - or 'The Jungle' as the ground is called today - in mid-January. Peter recalls that, late in a game where Saints were trailing (the only defeat in the sequence mentioned above), he picked up a Castleford knock-on and set off up field only for referee Peter Massey to blow his whistle and signal a scrum. Peter felt advantage would have been a more logical decision and he let the official have the benefit of his opinion - perhaps a little too enthusiastically, hence his 10 minute rest in the dressing room.

Peter had avoided the distinction of being the first player anywhere to try out the new law. That honour fell to Trevor Leathley and Clive Pickerill who, wasting no time, were binned during the Huddersfield versus Wakefield game on New Years Day.

The following week I caught up with Peter after the home win against Barrow and mentioned to him how impressed I had been with his try when he sprinted in from distance at the clubhouse end. "I think I must have had the wind behind me," he replied modestly.

The highlight of the run of form was the magnificent second round Challenge Cup win at Headingley against a very much in form Leeds team. It seemed St Helens were peaking at the right time. There was perhaps too much left to do to win the championship, but, again, the question was being asked - were Wembley's twin towers in sight?

The quarter finals of the Challenge Cup saw Featherstone Rovers visit Knowsley Road. Saints had famously come to grief in cup ties at Rovers' Post Office Road before now, and some still spoke of the 'Featherstone bogey', but Saints would surely be too good for their visitors. Rovers were having an indifferent season, but had lost only three of their last 11 games before the cup tie, so were in form.

Everyone loves an upset apart, of course, from those on the wrong end of it and after the match Saints supporters were left bitterly disappointed, while the fans from Yorkshire among the 6,125 supporters were understandably ecstatic. Centre John Gilbert who, a few years previously, had been good enough to represent Great Britain at under-24 level, did the most damage, scoring two tries in Rovers' 11-10 win. It was Featherstone's year; they went on to create an even bigger surprise at Wembley by beating the mighty Hull in arguably the biggest ever final upset at that time. Once redoubtable cup fighters, always redoubtable cup fighters, seemed to be the maxim.

Saints bounced back immediately with a mid-week win at Warrington but for the rest of the season the team could only boast a 50 per cent success rate in their remaining league games. One of these games, a low key affair really, sticks in Peter's mind. After a visit to Halifax with some of the worst weather the Pennines could produce, Peter recalls he lay in the bath with his kit still on, too cold and miserable to take it off, despite a 23-5 win. That was the day when the wind on the M62 was so strong the traffic had to crawl up the hill out of Lancashire in first gear. One Saints fan at the ground said: "It would be better to visit places like this in early autumn." "Or spring," another responded ironically. The match took place on 10 April.

Saints finished the season in fourth place in the table, eight points behind champions Hull. The top four finish, the first since 1978, represented an obvious improvement and earned a home tie in the Premiership. Unfortunately Widnes repeated their Easter Monday Knowsley Road success on their way to an unexpected final victory at Headingley against a Hull team which seemed to be making losing finals something of a habit.

Again the trophy cabinet was bare, but there had been an overall improvement. Peter's consistency again shone through, as he missed only five of the 42 games and registered nine tries. There was no doubt that he was one of the rocks on which forthcoming success would be built.

Battling for Saints at Knowsley Road (Photo: Courtesy Alex Service)

11. 1983-84: Not quite there

As well as the usual early season optimism, August 1983 brought some major rule changes, the two most significant of which were the handover and the four-point try. Previously after the sixth tackle teams would battle for possession via a scrum, but now the ball was to be automatically surrendered to the team which had completed the tackling stint. This meant tactical kicking became more important as teams sought field position and the chance to win the subsequent scrum if touch was found - far more preferable than simply handing the ball to their opponents. The number of scrums was reduced and as a result there seemed to be more continuity in the game.

A change in the scrummaging rules, whereby the non-offending team had both head and ball scrum advantage made scrums far more predictable and signalled the beginning of the end of the art of scrummaging and in the next 20 years the role of the hooker would totally alter. The rule changes brought about higher scores and enabled some mathematically-minded fans to convert 'new scores' into 'old scores' under the three-point try rule. It was a little like Britain adopting decimal currency all over again.

The honour of scoring the first four-point try for St Helens fell to Brian Parkes, a utility back. Playing at right centre his try helped Saints make a storming start to the season as they comfortably beat the previous season's runners-up and champions elect Hull Kingston Rovers at Knowsley Road.

The season began well with three wins, one of which, at Rochdale, was attended by probably the smallest crowd to see Peter in a St Helens jersey. As Hornets had a commitment to staging a stock car event on the Sunday the first round Lancashire Cup tie had to be staged on Saturday. Just 720 people turned up on a blustery and overcast afternoon in early September and saw Saints win easily at the Athletic Grounds, now of course demolished. Poor though the crowd was, only four of Rochdale's games attracted a bigger crowd that season and even though the team could only finish 12th in the Second Division it certainly deserved better support from the seemingly apathetic sporting public of the town.

That win enabled Saints to make progress in the Lancashire Cup and the second round saw what must be one of the stormiest matches ever staged at Knowsley Road. Holders Warrington were the visitors, but Saints with home advantage and having already won at Wilderspool in the league shortly beforehand were generally expected to progress. Warrington's approach might best be described as physical and five players were sent off - Mark Forster, Phil Ford and Mal Yates for Warrington as well as Roy Haggerty and Steve Peters for the home team. Warrington's Bob Eccles and Mike Gregory also visited the sin bin and, at one stage, Warrington were reduced to nine men. Despite numerical supremacy, Saints seemed unable to change tactics and adapt to the faster pace which the rule changes had generated and they lost 30-26.

Despite a 50-point thrashing of Wakefield Trinity in late September the team was struggling and indeed it took Peter until the start of October to register his first try of the season although the occasion - a big defeat at Oldham - signalled perhaps the worst display of the entire season and it holds no good memories. There were problems to be addressed and that week Peter lost his regular second-row partner Gary Moorby. He was transferred to Leeds in exchange for Tony Burke who would prove to be a model of consistency in Saints' front-row and, before too long, Peter's propping partner.

Tony Burke's arrival also heralded the departure of Welshman Mel James who made more than 300 appearances during his 11 years with the club. Mel had been an excellent servant since his arrival from Welsh rugby union in 1972, recovering well from a serious broken leg sustained against the Australians early in his career. "He was 'Mr Dependable'," said Peter, "a hard-working prop who was very quiet and unassuming."

'Buzzer' Burke made his debut in a home win against Fulham and proved to be something of a talisman as his new team, despite Peter's absence, performed really well to defeat league leaders Bradford Northern, again at Knowsley Road. Saints had picked up the pieces and embarked on a far better run, progressing to the John Player semi-finals in the process thanks to wins against Kent Invicta, Warrington and Featherstone. Was the Saints jinx surrounding that particular competition about to be broken? The team had reached the first three semi-finals of the competition - which began in 1971-72 - but had never gone further; a disappointing record for one of the game's biggest clubs.

Peter, however, found himself spending some time on the bench following the emergence of young back-row forwards like Andy Platt and Paul Round who had taken his place in the Bradford match. This would contribute to an inspired positional change for him later in the season.

Shortly before Christmas, Widnes ended Saints' interest in the John Player Trophy in the semi-final at Warrington and results again took a turn for the worse. The Boxing Day game at Wigan was lost narrowly by virtue of Wigan's Colin Whitfield kicking more goals than St Helens' Steve Rule, both teams scoring just one try. Saints' try in the 12-8 defeat came from Peter who, according to press reports, was one of the better players: "Saints' heroes were scrum-half Johnny Smith, second-rowers Andrew Platt and Peter Gorley plus foraging prop Tony Burke. Smith impressed many... he was superb."

Peter was certainly impressed by Smith who often had to act as Neil Holding's understudy but who, according to Peter, was a much underrated performer. "He was very loyal to Saints," said Peter, "because he could have got into many other first teams."

By the time bottom-of-the-table Whitehaven visited on a stormy afternoon in mid-January the unthinkable word 'relegation' was being bandied about in some quarters. The match against the Cumbrians was the first of three against teams below Saints in the table. One of the smallest crowds for many years at Knowsley Road saw the Cumbrians, without a win all season, easily beaten and then it was off to Fulham, who were also finding life difficult, for another crucial game.

The match was won in style, but Peter remembers it principally for the foul weather and the violent winter thunderstorm which broke over the ground as the players experienced four seasons and all manner of climatic excitement in one afternoon. Saints were far from feeling under the weather, though, as they recorded a convincing 30-0 win. The following week Salford were also nilled, and so all three vital games were won.

There was now less fear of following Wigan's fate in 1980 and dropping into the Second Division and it was that time of year when the Challenge Cup ties begin, renewing hope for many underachieving clubs. Saints were given a home derby against Leigh who had been struggling a little since they, too, had lost in their John Player semi-final, but the match was nevertheless a very appealing cup-tie to which both sets of fans were looking forward.

The win at Fulham more or less signalled the end of Paul Grimes' short, but successful Knowsley Road career, which would have a significant effect on Peter's season. He needed an operation on a knee injury and played only once more for Saints, in the following September, before moving to Workington Town. His absence meant that both props who began the season were now out of the picture. Who could successfully accompany Graham Liptrot and Tony Burke in the front-row? Would another foray into the transfer market be necessary?

Peter played prop in the team which came from behind to beat Leigh on 12 February. "Gorley was a tower of strength in midfield" read a press report as Saints came back from an early 10-point deficit to progress into the next round. His move to the number 10 jersey was to prove highly successful and it transformed his career.

The second round of the Challenge Cup saw history repeating itself from 1981. Again Hull visited, again the match was televised on a Saturday and again the Humberside fans were out in force, although the number of visitors this time was not overwhelming and there was no need for Saints fans to transfer to different parts of the ground. Again the teams were level on tries scored and again Saints won, thanks in no small measure to Harry Pinner's four drop-goals. If Hull, who would go on to finish championship runners-up, could be beaten, then why should Saints fear anyone?

The luck of the draw held with another home tie, with Saints' old friends from Central Park as the next scheduled visitors. "You should never bet on a Saints versus Wigan game," is an old saying, but the week before Saints warmed up with a fine win at Featherstone and their fans were all justifiably confident. Peter took his place both on the front of the programme cover, which praised his recent brilliant form and confirmed how well he had slotted into Paul Grimes's role, and in a St Helens team which looked too good for Wigan.

Adding to the occasion was the presence of former Saints legend Alex Murphy as coach on the visitors' bench. Having so often plotted Wigan's downfall in the past - older Wiganers remember his Wembley try against them in 1961 and his tactics and exploitation of the rules in 1966 at the same venue - he was now intent on knocking his home town team out of the Challenge Cup.

On a horrible, grim, wet day 20,007 fans assembled to watch the tie. The pitch was heavy, the ball was slippery and open rugby was at a premium. It always looked as though the first try would be crucial, and it fell to St Helens as Barry Ledger flew in at the corner. The match turned on a memorable blunder by Clive Griffiths who left his wing and kicked towards the area he had just vacated. Wigan took advantage of the open space to score and go in front. Saints heads seemed to drop and soon after Wigan scored again. Maybe they were flattered by the final score of 16-7 but they were in the semi-final. Peter and his team mates had missed out again.

Wigan's tries were scored by Australian stand-off Mark Cannon and substitute John Pendlebury, with Colin Whitfield adding four goals. Clive Griffiths added a goal and Neil Holding a drop-goal to Ledger's try.

Underneath the excitement of reaching the semi-final, Alex Murphy said he felt some disappointment - once a Saint, always a Saint - but it could not compare with that of Peter, the other players and the St Helens supporters.

Peter was now 32. He was playing magnificently, but perhaps he never would have the chance to play at Wembley.

The aftermath of that match was something of a test of character for the players but one with which they coped admirably. Until the end of the season they were defeated in only one of their remaining nine league games and they enjoyed some measure of revenge over Wigan by winning on Good Friday. A sixth-placed finish meant a trip to Warrington in the Premiership for the fifth meeting of the two clubs that season.

Perhaps memories of the Lancashire Cup tie were fresh in the mind, because there was no love lost between the teams, particularly in a physical, try-less first half punctuated with fouls and niggly exchanges. Saints played a more expansive style of rugby in the second half and won 19-13, thanks in no small measure to the contributions of prop forwards Peter Gorley and Tony Burke.

Carry on, Gorley

One newspaper headline after the Warrington game

Peter's performance had helped to postpone his pending retirement - at least for one more week. He had greatly enjoyed his time at St Helens but he was getting no younger and growing a little tired of the travelling to and from his home in Cockermouth. "I've had five years of travelling and I think it is sensible to go out at the top. I don't intend to play for any other club," he said, but his brilliant form in his new position had persuaded the club to ask him to change his mind. History shows Peter did change his mind - and what an inspired decision that was.

The good end-of-season form left the supporters in an optimistic frame of mind, albeit with an empty trophy cabinet once again. St Helens had a good team, but the squad wasn't quite there yet.

Peter's contribution was immense. Consistent as ever, he and Barry Ledger played more games than anyone else and supporters struggled when asked to name one of his bad games.

That was because bad games were very rare. It was time he was rewarded for his efforts on the field, the dedication he had shown to the club and his martyrdom to the M6 motorway.

12. 1984-85: Meninga the catalyst

'Good - but not quite there.' Saints supporters felt that something - or someone - was required to push the team that little bit further, for it was clear the potential was there. St Helens had good players, of that there was no doubt. There was a promising blend of youth and experience, and a good quota of locals who were proud to represent their home town on the rugby pitch. An extra ingredient would probably transform the team into trophy winners and help bring Peter the medals he so richly deserved.

The St Helens board reckoned it knew who was needed and Mal Meninga had announced in March 1984 that he would like to play for an English club. Ahead of the 1984 Great Britain tour of Australia one of Saints' directors, John Clegg, had done much preparatory work to bring about the star signing from the Antipodes. It was to be a massive coup - one of the biggest signings in the St Helens club's history.

The key man in the negotiations was Ray French, the former Saints forward who was following the tour while working for the BBC. The paperwork had been completed. Ray had to contact and sign Mal Meninga.

It did not prove easy. Australia is a huge country and your target may be in a city hundreds of miles away. Ray French recalls being under pressure for two months to complete the signing. Happily, Saints' man was up to the task. Although Leeds and Wigan were also in the chase, Mal gave his word over the phone to Ray that he would sign and, being a man of honour, he kept it. He became a Saint in June 1984, and during his time at Knowsley Road developed a firm friendship with Peter.

He was one of a number of Australian greats from that era to grace the British game. Wigan had flying winger John Ferguson and star stand-off Brett Kenny who made everything look so easy. Leeds obtained the services of 'rolling thunder' Eric Grothe, a quick, massive wingman who became a prolific try scorer during his stay at Headingley. Peter Sterling, one of the finest scrum-halves ever produced by Australia, signed for Hull. Who was the best signing? The Knowsley Road fraternity was in no doubt.

Mal also brought a friend with him to keep him company during his short stay, who had also been signed by Ray French. He was a young player who, supporters were told, could play full-back or winger (although they subsequently found out that he could play virtually anywhere) and he would be a useful acquisition for the coming season although he was not expected to stay longer than that. In fact he went on to play nearly 400 games for the club and he became a huge fans' favourite as well as a priceless asset because of his utility value. He particularly impressed the fans with his ability to deal with 'up-and-unders' - or 'bombs' as the new terminology would have it. Phil Veivers' time at Saints was a wonderful spin off to the signing of Mal Meninga.

Phil recalls he had problems understanding Peter when they first met: "The main thing I remember about Peter was that his accent was the hardest to understand – I always had to ask someone else to tell me what he'd said. I always got on well with him and I remember a night out with him and Mal [Meninga] in Cockermouth when Peter demonstrated his liking for Cumbrian ale. He was an uncompromising forward who always put in a good stint and did the hard work so that the backs could shine. His name was one of the first on the team sheet each week. He was as tough as teak but one of the game's gentlemen as well. He was good for the club in that his experience helped younger players such as Paul Forber and Bernard Dwyer to develop into quality forwards."

Before the arrival of the Australian duo, Saints fans were able to welcome another new face to the club. Indeed, that was his name for a while – he followed the time-honoured practice of using AN Other during a trial period - before he was finally revealed to be Sean Day, goal-kicking machine extraordinaire and one-season wonder. But what a season: he scored 157 goals for the club and, as Mal's winger, ran in 12 tries. A subsequent serious shoulder injury meant he disappeared almost as suddenly as he had appeared and he later moved on to Runcorn Highfield but in 1984-85 he was a key man, and what memories he took with him.

The season began with great expectations, but without the new Australians who were scheduled to arrive in early October. The fixture list looked daunting with trips to Bradford, Leeds and Hull

Kingston Rovers among the first four league games. Nevertheless, Saints made a good start beating Featherstone and Leeds in the league and Runcorn Highfield in the Lancashire Cup before suffering two league defeats in Yorkshire. However a good win at Barrow in the Lancashire Cup allowed Saints progress in that competition. By now Peter was regarded as a prop, although he had reverted to second-row at Barrow, but he was as mobile as ever and enjoyed an early season sequence of three tries in four games.

When Mal arrived the team had a 50 per cent success record in the league, but fans expected the team to kick on under the influence of the new recruit. They weren't disappointed. Mal first played for the Saints at home to Castleford at the start of October. The attendance increased immediately as more than 7,000 fans made their way to Knowsley Road - 3,000 more than had seen the first match against Featherstone. They saw Mal explode into action with two tries and two goals as Castleford were beaten 30-16. The only slight disappointment was Mal's goal-kicking, but with young Sean Day available it didn't seem to matter. After all, Mal could do everything else you would expect a man to do on a rugby field and Saints were flying.

Saints reached the Lancashire Cup Final after a great semi-final win against Leigh a few days after the Castleford match. There was a chance that Peter's medal drought with Saints was about to come to an end. On the same night that Saints beat Leigh, when Mal scored another try and a couple of goals and 2,000 extra fans appeared from nowhere and found their way to Knowsley Road, Wigan beat Salford in the other semi-final. The expectation for the Lancashire Cup Final was immense.

The meeting of two big and neighbouring rivals created a problem though: where should the match be played? Was there a venue large enough to accommodate the expected crowd?

Warrington's Wilderspool Stadium was suggested, but Saints and Wigan both felt with justification that its 16,000 capacity would not be enough. It was agreed that the match should be played at St Helens or Wigan, to be decided on the toss of a coin. The coin came down in Wigan's favour.

Form in the biggest of all rugby derby matches often goes out of the window, and frequently the away team seems to do well. Even in season 1969-70 when Saints recorded a spectacular 53-11 win at Central Park on Boxing Day, Wigan won the return match on Good Friday quite comfortably. Nevertheless, a trip to Central Park appeared daunting even though Saints, on a fine run of form - five successive wins, topping 30 points on each occasion - seemed to be pre-match favourites.

On Sunday 28 October (the first Lancashire Cup Final to be held on the Sabbath) more than 26,000 fans, the majority of them Wiganers, assembled on a gloomy and misty afternoon. A sensational first half performance, orchestrated by Mal, won the cup for St Helens. He was unstoppable and merciless on a young Wigan full-back called Shaun Edwards who, cast in the role of David, could not cope with the Australian Goliath. Meninga scored the first try then sent Roy Haggerty, who had come on for concussion victim Phil Veivers, over for another touchdown. The Australian superstar then made a try for Sean Day before he sprinted round David Stephenson and Shaun Edwards - neither of them slow players - to score again: 24-2 was the unbelievable half time score.

It couldn't become any worse for Wigan; they were surely going to fight back and they did. Matters were radically different after the interval, recalls Peter, as Wigan appeared to have all the possession. "It was a real backs to the wall effort," he says. "I remember we had to put in a massive tackling stint to win the game." Although Wigan recovered well they had too much to do and Saints won the trophy for the first time since 1968. It was also the first trophy of any sort since the 1977 Premiership.

The excitement was all too much for one supporter. When the lap of honour reached the place opposite his 'spot' on the terraces he was away, over the wall and running round with the victorious team. The long arm of the law kindly left him to it, although I'm sure I heard one policeman ask his colleague: "Who's that big bloke with the beard and that splendid shiny trophy running round with Pete Cropper?"

As well as scoring a try, Sean Day kicked five goals to add to Meninga's two tries and Haggerty's effort. For Wigan, Henderson Gill,

Graeme West and Nicky Kiss scored tries and Colin Whitfield kicked three goals. The referee was Ron Campbell from Widnes.

St Helens: Veivers; Ledger, Allen, Meninga, Day; Arkwright, Holding; Burke, Liptrot, Gorley, Platt, Round, Pinner.
Subs: Smith, Haggerty.

Wigan: Edwards; Ferguson, Stephenson, Whitfield, Gill; Cannon, Fairhurst; Courtney, Kiss, Case, West, Wane, Potter.
Subs: Pendlebury, Scott.

The teams from the programme for the Lancashire Cup Final.
(Courtesy: Rugby Football League)

ST. HELENS		WIGAN
Blue Jerseys White Shorts		Cherry and White hooped jerseys White Shorts
Coach: Billy Benyon		Coach: Colin Clarke / Alan McInnes
Phil Vievers	1	Shaun Edwards
Barrie Ledger	2	John Ferguson
Shaun Allen	3	David Stephenson
Mal Meninga	4	Colin Whitfield
Sean Day	5	Henderson Gill
Chris Arkwright	6	Mark Cannon
Neil Holding	7	Jimmy Fairhurst
Tony Burke	8	Neil Courtney
Graham Liptrot	9	Nicky Kiss
Peter Gorley	10	Brian Case
Andy Platt	11	Graeme West
Paul Round	12	Shaun Wayne
Harry Pinner	13	Ian Potter
Steve Peters	14	John Pendlebury
Roy Haggerty	15	Mick Scott

'Big Mal' was the obvious hero but in the programme for the next home game against Barrow, fans were informed that in the voting for the 'McEwan-Younger Player of the Month' award where the opposing coach at each match awarded points for the players he considered to be Saints' top performers, Wigan's joint coaches - Colin Clarke and Alan McInnes - had decided Peter was man-of-the- match for his unsung heroism in the Saints pack that day.

Of course the triumph brought back great memories for Peter of another final triumph against Wigan in the same competition. Basking in the glory of it all he, with Shaun Edwards, was the last in the post-match bath. Young Shaun was talking with Peter about the

Wigan full-back's new deal; it was a great contract for a youngster, but in order to pick up all that he'd been promised, it was dependent upon him captaining Great Britain. No matter how much potential a young player had, there was no guarantee that he would make the grade. But the rest, as they say, is history. Edwards went on to captain Great Britain and more. "In my view," says Peter, "he earned every penny he got." Whether you like Shaun Edwards or not, it would be difficult to disagree.

With the season's first trophy safely on the sideboard, Saints stormed on, rattling up some huge scores with an open, expansive style of play. Lightning fast Barry Ledger registered try hat-tricks in successive weeks in November and Peter bagged his fifth try of the season in the middle of the same month. Having beaten Bradford in the league and then knocked them out of the John Player Trophy, a ruthless second-half destruction of a powerful Leeds team in early December was particularly pleasing and memorable. When Halifax, a team of willing, committed but largely unknown Australians, arrived for the quarter-final of the John Player Trophy just before Christmas, Saints had gone 13 games unbeaten - a sequence which had begun on Mal's debut.

Halifax's form had been erratic, but what a funny game rugby league can be. The home team, completely out of sorts, lost 14-8.

Further disappointment came on Boxing Day when, despite Peter roaring in for a great try (his fifth in Saints' colours against Wigan), Saints lost again in front of more than 17,000 fans at Knowsley Road. It was hardly a Merry Christmas - would it be a Happy New Year for St Helens? A cup run culminating in a Wembley trip would do nicely for all at the club particularly Peter who felt this was perhaps his last chance.

Form was sketchy and there had been reports of unrest in the camp. It was not ideal preparation for a cup tie against league leaders Hull Kingston Rovers although Saints did have home advantage. The game fell victim to the weather and was played on a Thursday night in February, when just a few more than 9,000 people saw Peter's Wembley hopes disappear again as Rovers' winger Garry Clark scored the only try and edged his team home in a very tight match.

St Helens players with the Lancashire Cup after the victory against Wigan.
Paul Round, Neil Holding and Barry Ledger with the Cup, Peter is behind
Andy Platt and Sean Day (Photo: Courtesy Alex Service)

St Helens with the Lancashire Cup before beating Keighley 60-8 on
18 November 1984. Peter is third from the left in the back row, next to
Mal Meninga. (Photo: Courtesy Alex Service)

It was hard for Peter to hide his disappointment. "I thought this was going to be Saints' year," he said later. "If we'd have beaten Hull Kingston Rovers and then won against Rochdale, who Rovers faced next, we'd have been in the quarter-final and well on the road to Wembley. But it wasn't to be and we're left to reflect on what might have been. When we were leading 3-2 I thought the match was ours - but Rovers caught us and nipped in for the all-important match-winning try."

Shortly afterwards the club suffered another blow when hooker Graham Liptrot broke his jaw at Featherstone. This, the fourth such injury in his career, finished his season. Some thought it would finish his career, but he was made of sterner stuff. He was to be replaced most adequately by Gary Ainsworth, on loan from Leigh. The new man was particularly lively in the loose and he added a new dimension to Saints' attacking play.

After a spell of mixed fortunes away from home with two wins and two defeats, the next home game saw Peter's old team visit, but although Workington had gained promotion the previous season the team was nowhere near strong enough to survive and the Derwent Park decline was obvious and sad to see. Although Peter says there was never any room for sentiment when playing against his former club, he must have had mixed feelings. He was one of nine try scorers in a thoroughly one-sided 62-0 win achieved despite stand-in hooker Paul Forber losing the scrums 15-3 against Workington's John Banks - cousin of Alan Banks who was, of course, number nine at Derwent Park during Peter's time there. Town's glory days must to their supporters have seemed decades rather than a few years ago and, apart from successive Old Trafford Divisional Premiership appearances, a Third and a Second Division Championship in that same period and a brief flirtation with Super League in 1996, the club is still looking to recapture the successes of yesteryear. A crowd of just 3,583 saw the Workington game, illustrating the fickleness of sports fans.

The win spurred Saints on and they were to lose only one more league game - a surprising defeat at relegated Leigh. Included in the sequence was Good Friday revenge at Wigan's Central Park, perhaps not unexpected bearing in mind the discussion earlier about home advantage - or otherwise - in the big derby matches. Wigan had their minds on Wembley whereas Saints didn't - or so it was claimed in some quarters.

I recall on my approach to the ground noticing a tall, familiar looking figure waiting outside. Although by nature not a liar, I was a little embarrassed at my age - 28 - to ask one of my favourites for his autograph, so it wasn't for me, it was for 'my little lad'. Peter has since forgiven me.

Saints finished second, their highest position since 1977. Their entertaining brand of rugby meant they were comfortably the top points scorers in the division, setting a new First Division record in the process, although they also conceded a lot of points - but that is the St Helens style. It meant they were in the mood to have a concerted effort at the Premiership.

Near the end of the season, in the programme for the Hull match, when Saints played superbly to thrash one of the top teams of the day, programme writer Neil Barker gave his assessment of the squad's performances through the season. Of Peter he wrote: "A truly great forward. The gentle giant who's been a revelation since his move from Workington. Never lets the side down and hopefully youngsters have learned from his attitude and style."

The first round Premiership tie was against Widnes and home fans were delighted not only by the comfortable victory - a little surprising after two close games in the league - but also by the announcement in the programme that coach Billy Benyon had been offered a new contract. Next up in the semi-final was Wigan, the 'old enemy', fresh from a Wembley Challenge Cup Final win against Hull the previous weekend.

They may have been fresh from victory, but they were physically tired. Typically sporting, Peter declared that the arrangement was not really fair on Wigan - but the Saints fans at Knowsley Road didn't seem to want to spring to their visitors' defence.

Events surrounding the game provide one of Peter's most vivid memories of his St Helens career. As usual, match day began with a long drive south and he set off from Broughton at his usual time, but this did not take into account the large amount of traffic pouring out of Wigan towards the end of his journey. Having left the M6, Peter was caught up in heavy traffic and he recalls crawling along to the East Lancashire Road, anxiously looking at his watch. Time was running out. He tried all the short cuts he knew, but eventually he had to concede that he didn't really know where he was. He had no choice other than to abandon the car in Ruskin Drive and to run to the ground, following the crowds and relying on those whose local knowledge was better than his. He arrived in the changing room at 7.15pm, pouring with sweat, a mere 15 minutes before kick-off, and he was pleased to see his jersey still on the peg. Billy Benyon wasn't flustered - he had every confidence that his star prop would arrive on time. These days, of course, a mobile phone would have taken some of the stress out of the situation.

After his quick-change act, Peter went out and gave his usual great performance that the supporters were now taking for granted. The match was close for a time, but Saints pulled away late on to record a great 37-14 win to set up a final date with Hull Kingston Rovers at Elland Road.

Peter stayed overnight for a photo call the following day ahead of the club tour to New Zealand at the end of the season and then came the real challenge - locating his car. With local assistance it was found in about half an hour.

Premiership Final

The Premiership Final against the Champions and Premiership holders at Elland Road provided one of the highlights of Peter's time at Saints and in a quite magnificent match Saints defeated Rovers 36-16, a then record score in the Premiership Final.

Saints got off to a flying start with Peter instrumental in the move that saw Gary Ainsworth register an early try. Prompted by star loose-forward Harry Pinner who was magnificent all afternoon, Saints played some brilliant rugby and scored three more tries, through Phil Veivers, Barry Ledger and Mal Meninga, to lead 22-14 at half time.

A second-half penalty by George Fairbairn put Rovers just one score behind and they were on the attack when the game's defining moment arrived. For the second time in the match Mal Meninga intercepted a long pass from David Hall and this time he tore along the touchline for 80 yards with Rovers' flying winger Garry Clark in hot, but vain, pursuit. Some had said Meninga lacked a little pace. They were proved to be very wrong.

The try broke the Champions' resistance and Harry Pinner strolled through a gap for a deserved try before another bout of brilliant passing created Barry Ledger's second touchdown.

Every one of the team was a hero that day and captain Harry Pinner deservedly took the Harry Sunderland Trophy as man-of-the-match but everybody present recalls Mal's two interceptions. It goes without saying that Peter gave his usual 100 per cent performance in the pack which helped to lay the foundations for victory.

Chris Arkwright recalls Peter's contribution to Saints' victory: "I knew I'd done a good tackling stint, and after the match I looked to see how many tackles I'd made," he remembers. "My total was high, but not as high as Peter's. This sums up his commitment and attitude. People remember Mal's two interception tries, but to my mind Peter won the Premiership for Saints that day."

Harry Pinner, who was the linchpin of the St Helens team during Peter's time at the club, believes that this match, with the Lancashire Cup victory earlier in the season, was the highlight of his and Peter's time at the club. He recognised Peter's consistent efforts for the team: "You always got 110 per cent from Peter Gorley," he said. "He'd always take the ball up and you would never hear him moan or complain. You'd get exactly the same effort from him week after week. He was a typically hard, gritty Cumbrian forward, and a naturally fit lad."

St Helens: Veivers; Ledger, Peters, Meninga, Day; Arkwright, Holding; Burke, Ainsworth, Gorley, Platt, Haggery, Pinner. Subs: Allen, Forber.

Hull Kingston Rovers: Fairbairn; Clark, Robinson, Prohm, Laws; M. Smith, G. Smith; Broadhurst Watkinson, Ema, Kelly, Hogan, Hall. Subs: Harkin, Lydiat.

Sean Day landed four goals for Saints, while for Hull Kingston Rovers, Fairbairn, Laws and Robinson scored tries, and Fairbairn added two goals.

Action from the Premiership Final against Hull Kingston Rovers
(Photo: Courtesy Alex Service)

St Helens captain Harry Pinner holds the Premiership Trophy after the victory
against Hull Kingston Rovers.
(Photo: Courtesy Alex Service)

HULL K.R.		ST. HELENS
Red jersey with blue band		Two-tone blue jersey
Coach: **ROGER MILLWARD M.B.E.**		Coach: **BILLY BENYON**
George Fairbairn	**1**	Phil Veivers
Garry Clark	**2**	Barry Ledger
Ian Robinson	**3**	Steve Peters
Gary Prohm	**4**	Mal Meninga
David Laws	**5**	Sean Day
Mike Smith	**6**	Chris Arkwright
~~Paul Harkin~~/Gordon Smith	**7**	Neil Holding
Mark Broadhurst	**8**	Tony Burke
David Watkinson, (Captain)	**9**	Gary Ainsworth
Asuquo Ema	**10**	Peter Gorley
Andy Kelly	**11**	Andy Platt
Phil Hogan	**12**	Roy Haggerty
David Hall	**13**	Harry Pinner, (Captain)
HARKIN	**14**	Shaun Allen
LYDIAT	**15**	Paul Forber

The teams from the programme for the Premiership Final
(Courtesy Rugby Football League)

Stan Wall officiated in what was his last match before compulsory retirement on age grounds. Nearly 20 years later he is an active, well-liked figure at Knowsley Road as kit man. The attendance was 15,518 which was perhaps rather disappointing given the quality of both sides.

Some observers rated this triumph and the overall standard of the match as better even than the previous week's Wembley classic between Wigan and Hull. Yet amid the euphoria of victory were concerns. Mal Meninga was not returning the following year. He had promised to come back at a later date although fate decreed that a broken arm would prevent that happening, but could he be replaced in the short term? If Mal wasn't returning, had the team - arguably one of the best Saints teams - gone as far as it could?

While supporters were considering these questions on the way home, news came through of the appalling tragedy at nearby Valley Parade, Bradford City's football ground, at which 56 people died when the main stand burned down. This put all our musing into awful perspective. It was only a game we were worrying about.

St Helens had had a wonderful season, of that there was no doubt, and it was equally obvious that Peter had played his part fully. His coach, Billy Benyon, said: "Peter has played very well this season. I couldn't have asked for any more from him. He has led by example and is a true professional." His captain, Harry Pinner, said: "He is a tremendous player and all of us respect him. His dedication to Saints over the years has been fantastic and I know how much a Wembley win would mean to him." Sadly, it would never happen.

Peter's view at this stage was: "I don't regret coming to Saints because they're a great club. I've enjoyed every minute of my spell here and just wish I'd come sooner. I've played alongside some terrific players and there's a great atmosphere in the camp... Bill Benyon is one of the best coaches I've played under and he's done well getting us to this level."

At the end of the wonderful campaign it was a great thrill for the players to undertake a club tour of New Zealand. Peter particularly enjoyed it: "It was the best trip ever - three weeks with very good friends. Who could fail to have a good time?"

A publicity photo for the New Zealand tour
(Photo: Courtesy Alex Service)

Peter recalls that he roomed with Harry Pinner and the room was always such a mess they ended up having a collection for the cleaner who was prepared to tidy, wash and iron while the team were having a good time. Peter and Harry's packed schedule unfortunately did not permit time for domestics.

On the field, Saints lost three games before winning the last one in some style. Peter missed the first two defeats against Canterbury, 30-24, and Waikato, 34-24, but he played in the third game against Manukau. The Saints team that day was: Loughlin; Ledger, Allen, Peters, Day; Arkwright, Holding; Round, Ainsworth, Gorley, Platt, Haggerty, Pinner. Subs: Veivers, Wellens. Paul Round scored the try and Sean Day kicked three goals as Saints lost 26-10.

The next day saw the following team line up against Northland: Wellens; Ledger, Pinner, Loughlin, Holding; Allen, Smith; Gorley, Ainsworth, Arkwright, Platt, Haggerty, Peters. Subs: Veivers, Round. Saints tries in a 42-12 win were scored by Shaun Allen, who picked up three, Paul Loughlin, Neil Holding, Andy Platt, Roy Haggerty and Peter who also added a goal - the only one he kicked for St Helens - to add to four goals by Loughlin. The team sheets showed one or two less familiar names such as young Paul Loughlin who would go on to score more than 800 goals and 2,000 points in almost 300 full appearances for Saints and full-back Kevin Wellens, an able deputy for Phil Veivers. The name Wellens is recognisable to fans of the Super League era as Kevin's younger brother Paul would wear the number one jersey with distinction nearly 20 years later.

13. 1985-86: All good things...

The 1984-85 season had, of course, been the best at Knowsley Road for some time. League runners-up plus two trophies on the sideboard was a record of which any club would have been proud. Two players - Ledger and Meninga - were among the game's top five try scorers and, in wingman Day, Saints had the top goal-kicker. Captain Harry Pinner's brilliance consistently shone through.

Yet two heroes - often unsung - stood out when the end-of-season statistics are studied carefully. Peter and fellow prop Tony Burke both played more than 40 times, Peter missing only one game and his front-row colleague being ever-present. These highly consistent players were the backbone of the side. Peter's efforts were recognised by fans throughout the county as he won the Lancashire Federation of Supporters Clubs' player-of-the-year trophy. It is also worth bearing in mind that, unlike in Super League, prop forwards were generally expected to play a full 80 minutes. Peter seldom failed to finish a game which he started.

This was a great effort from a player whose original intention had been to retire in 1984. It would have cost him so much and similarly his contribution would have been greatly missed by everyone at the club. At the end of 1984-85 he again considered retirement very seriously but was persuaded to carry on by Billy Benyon.

But his Saints career couldn't last for ever and, as the old saying goes: "All good things must come to an end."

The 1985-86 season began with some good results. Coach Billy Benyon had agreed a new two-year contract and five out of the first six games were won, as the team reached the semi-final of the Lancashire Cup. There was no Mal Meninga and, at the start of the season, no Phil Veivers, so Paul Loughlin had opportunities to shine at full-back. Supporters were looking forward to the arrival of three Australians - prop Gary Greinke and centres Ross Conlon and Brett French who, it was hoped, would offset the loss of Meninga.

However, there were some problems. Wrongly in the view of many supporters, the club had not retained Gary Ainsworth after his loan period and he returned to Hilton Park even though Graham Liptrot was still not fit. This gave Dave Harrison a chance to stake a claim at hooker and he didn't let the team down although he lacked Ainsworth's great flair in the loose. Other injuries to key players, notably Harry Pinner, affected the team. Games were being won, but neither fluently nor comfortably.

Saints' defence of the Lancashire Cup began with a 72-8 home game win against Carlisle, just short of the club record score of 73-0 against Wardley in 1924. Further progress was made when Whitehaven, complete with Les Gorley in the front-row, also returned disappointed to Cumbria. However, problems lay ahead.

By the time the Lancashire Cup semi-final against Wigan at Central Park was played, Saints certainly had injury worries. Although Phil Veivers's return from Australia was an obvious bonus, Harry Pinner was still missing and the young and inexperienced Bernard Dwyer was drafted into the role of hooker. Never in contention, Saints suffered a big defeat, 30-2, that grim Wednesday evening and lost their grip on the trophy. Clearly all was not well.

Champions Hull Kingston Rovers were convincingly beaten at Knowsley Road, 39-22, to suggest better times were round the corner but three weeks later, in a game Peter missed, Saints were humiliated 46-8 by the New Zealand tourists - ironically undone by, among other things, the pace of centre Mark Elia who was to have a memorable career himself at Knowsley Road. Soon afterwards, in a move that some people felt smacked of desperation, Billy Benyon was sacked - paying, some people thought, for the club's failure to find a top-line replacement for Mal Meninga.

Peter had worked well with Billy. He was now 34 and obviously was not going to continue for much longer. It was possible that he would not fit into a new coach's plans. To this end, looking to future possibilities, he had begun coaching at Broughton Red Rose where it had all started for him. Like many players, he enjoyed putting something back into the game that had given him so much.

The new coach was Alex Murphy whose arrival provoked Biblical analogies. To some he was 'The Messiah', to others 'The Prodigal Son'. He was the man who was set to steady the ship and bring the good times back.

Peter and his new coach had contrasting styles. Alex Murphy's standing in the game was legendary. Arguably the greatest scrum-half ever, his playing career had been littered with success. Always outspoken whether as player or coach, he could never keep quiet and his comments were often controversial. Peter had a much more taciturn demeanour and he preferred to shun the limelight. Alex Murphy's approach was also different from that of Billy Benyon. It appeared there were changes afoot.

In the early days of Alex's reign Saints progressed to the semi-final of the John Player Trophy but, according to the club programme for the quarter-final tie against Hull: "...Saints have so far failed to impress. Their old habits still haunt them..." As if to answer this, the team produced a brilliant display to score more than 50 points against their powerful visitors and set up a semi-final date with Hull's Humberside neighbours.

The team approached the semi-final with confidence. Murphy's team had not lost since his appointment, and was on a nine match unbeaten run, Australian Brett French had settled in with nine tries since his arrival and, true to his pedigree, fellow Australian centre Ross Conlon was kicking goals from anywhere and everywhere. "But," said some supporters, "Saints have a habit of letting you down when you are expecting great things."

The wheels came off against Hull Kingston Rovers. The match was at a neutral venue - Headingley - and, on the Saturday before Christmas, a miserable crowd of 3,856 saw Saints fail to register a try in losing 22-4.

This began a sequence of six successive losses, included in which were big festive derby defeats against Wigan and Widnes. The 18-8 loss against Bradford at Knowsley Road in mid-January was the nadir and questions were even being asked about Saints' ability to remain in the top flight.

Two weeks later the rot was stopped as Featherstone were convincingly beaten at Knowsley Road. Peter began the match on the bench, replacing Chris Arkwright in what was to be his last appearance for the club.

Peter's Saints career ended unfortunately and somewhat acrimoniously; it was a very unsuitable way for one of the club's most reliable performers to depart. The Challenge Cup draw had produced an away tie at Dewsbury, but it was impossible to stage the match at Crown Flatt on the original date of 9 February owing to harsh winter weather. The Rugby League gave Dewsbury a deadline by which the tie would have to be played at their home ground, but if the weather did not relent it was stipulated that the match would have to be moved to Headingley with its undersoil heating. The freeze continued and, despite animated protests from Dewsbury, the protagonists gathered in Leeds on the evening of Monday, 24 February. As ever, the match necessitated a long drive, in wintry conditions, for Peter who, when Saints were playing in Yorkshire, would link up with the party at Birch Services on the M62 near Rochdale.

When he arrived at the ground, assistant coach Dave Chisnall read out the team and Peter discovered he wasn't playing - he hadn't even secured a place on the substitutes' bench. Obviously there was disappointment but there was anger too. Why could he have not been told earlier to save a long journey down from Cumbria? Why did assistant coach Dave Chisnall rather than Alex Murphy break the news? If it was deemed necessary for Peter to travel down that evening, could he not have been told quietly of his omission from the team on the coach on the way to Yorkshire? After the match Alex Murphy returned to St Helens by car rather than on the team coach and Peter was therefore unable to confront him.

Saints struggled to win the tie 22-19 against their opponents who eventually finished bottom of the First Division.

Peter was disappointed in Alex Murphy's man management techniques and he felt he should have been better treated. He had played a lot of matches and travelled a lot of miles for St Helens and to finish in the way he did left a nasty taste. If Peter was no longer in the coach's plans, he would have liked to have been told properly.

Annoyed and upset, Peter never played for Saints again. He was a loss, of that there was no doubt; in the programme for the Featherstone game he was in third place in the supporters' club player-of-the-season competition. He may have been at the veteran stage but he could still cut it at the top level.

Peter had, in any case, intended to retire at the end of the season and so for a while it seemed as though he had played his last game of professional rugby league, but he was tempted later in the season to follow his brother to the Recreation Ground for a short swansong with the Whitehaven club. On Good Friday he made his debut for Whitehaven, ironically in an Easter derby at Workington where it had all begun nearly 11 years earlier. He made his third winning debut in club rugby as his new team beat his first club 12-10 to record a league double over its keenest rivals.

Peter had turned 35 by the time the next season began. Father time was starting to catch up with him; he became increasingly plagued by back problems and, with the greatest of respect to Whitehaven, he felt he had taken a backwards step by moving to the Second Division. He was to play only two more games. His retirement came after a trip to Tattersfield, Doncaster on 12 October, 1986. Unfortunately, Peter was unable to finish with a victory and 743 spectators saw the home team win 28-12. After a grand total of 361 club appearances he called it a day.

A couple of Peter's team mates from his time with St Helens recognise his skill and commitment. Scrum-half Neil Holding said: "Peter was a true pro in every meaning of the word. He was quietly spoken off the field, but a rock of strength on it. Peter was probably one of the best second row forwards I played with; he had the ability to reach around an opponent and slip the ball to his supporting team mates which was me most of the time. On one occasion we were playing towards the restaurant end of Knowsley road and Peter was just held up short of the line with four opposing players around him, as I went to go in at the play the ball to my amazement the ball was in my arms and all I did was fall over the line for a try. George Nicholls, one of the best British post-war forwards, added: "I was an established first team player at Knowsley Road when Peter arrived from Workington and he quickly became a good friend of mine. Off the field he was a quiet, unassuming and contented person, but on the field he was quite different. He always wanted to play and he gave 100 per cent commitment to St Helens, never shirking his responsibilities with a work rate which was second to none. He was a tremendous tackler and he would take the ball forward all day. He was exactly the type of player around whom a team should be built - a pack with two or three Peter Gorleys in it would be just about ideal.

Peter was always very competitive; it must run in the family, as his brother Les also had a great career with Workington and Widnes. Both brothers were highly respected throughout the game."

Harry Pinner added: "You always got 110 per cent from Peter Gorley. He'd always take the ball up and you would never hear him moan or complain. You'd get exactly the same effort from him week after week. He was a typically hard, gritty Cumbrian forward, and a naturally fit lad."

14. Representative rugby

When he signed for Workington Town, Peter had been disappointed that he had not represented his country at amateur level. There was, however, still the chance to do so at professional level if he were good enough. And playing for Cumbria possibly alerts the international selectors. That was his first target.

Selection for county, then country, obviously relies upon consistently good performances at club level and Peter's outstanding efforts in the Workington pack after promotion to the First Division made county selection inevitable. He made his Cumbria debut on 5 October 1977 in the team which faced Yorkshire at Clarence Street, York, which is now, sadly, a housing estate. The result was a disappointment, Yorkshire winning 28-10, but Peter made his mark by scoring one of the tries, the other coming from Whitehaven's Gordon Cottier. The Cumbrian team for Peter's debut in representative rugby was:

Charlton (Workington); McConnell (Barrow), Wilkins (Workington), Risman (Workington), Collister (Workington); Mason (Barrow), Jones (Barrow); McCourt (Barrow), McCurrie (Whitehaven), Bowman (Workington), P. Gorley (Workington), Gainford (Whitehaven), P. Hogan (Barrow). Sub: Cottier. Phil Hogan kicked Cumbria's two goals and 2,633 watched the match.

His next Cumbrian appearance came a year later at Barrow when nearly 6,000 spectators gathered to see Cumbria challenge the might of the touring Australians. The Kangaroos were beginning an era of dominance over British teams and only Warrington, Widnes and Great Britain were able to beat the tourists in 1978. The match at Craven Park was the second of the tour following the opening game at the seaside against Blackpool Borough and the tourists, anxious to make a good early impression, won 47-4.

Boxer Walker remembers an amusing mistake from the match programme where a misprint conveyed the information that Peter was 45 years old; perhaps the prospect of facing the Australians might provoke premature ageing in some players, but nearly 20 years in one day would be rather ridiculous. On one of the many occasions when the Cumbrians were lining up behind the posts after a try to watch a conversion attempt, one of the spectators was heard to shout, "Aye, Gorley, you're playing as if you're 45 as well." It remains a standing joke between them to this day

Peter's last match for Cumbria in 1982 was remarkably similar as another crowd of just under 6,000, this time at Carlisle, saw the Australians, leading 16-2 at half time, win 41-2. Peter, Ralph McConnell, Mel Mason and Alan McCurrie were the only survivors from the last time the Kangaroos had visited the county.

Cumbria: Hopkins (Workington); Mackie (Whitehaven), Bell (Carlisle), McConnell (Barrow), Moore (Barrow); Mason (Barrow), Cairns (Barrow); Herbert (Barrow), McCurrie (Oldham), Flynn (Barrow), W. Pattinson (Workington), P. Gorley (St Helens), Hadley (Barrow) Subs: Beck (Workington), Hartley (Workington).

Australia: Brentnall; Boustead, Meninga, Ella, Ribot; Lewis, Sterling; McKinnon, Krilich, Hancock, Muggleton, Schubert, Pearce. Subs: Rogers, Price.

The qualification rules for Cumbria had changed some years previously and the team featured a Welshman (Lynn Hopkins), a Yorkshireman (Mel Mason) and even a Kiwi (Dean Bell), but they were eligible to play because they represented Cumbrian clubs. On paper the Cumbrian team was quite strong but these Australian tourists were record breaking Invincibles and the first tourists ever to return home undefeated. They gave British rugby league the most severe wake up call it had ever received.

Australia's tries were scored by Ribot, who scored twice, Meninga, Ella, Boustead, Sterling, McKinnon, Pearce and Rogers. Peter's future team mate and friend Meninga added seven goals. Hopkins scored Cumbria's goal. It was perhaps just as well that Alan McCurrie won the scrums 15-6.

The best performers, according to the *Evening News and Star* were David Cairns and Peter Gorley: "...former Workington man Gorley was the nearest Cumbria had to an Australian-type forward - breaking well and cleverly releasing the ball in the tackle." Overall, however, it was a disappointing state of affairs in Cumbria and county rugby league president Jack Atkinson called for more rugby league to be played in schools to re-establish the game at grass roots level.

98

In between times, when the team wasn't playing against super humans who nobody in the northern hemisphere could handle, Peter enjoyed a very successful county career.

Ten days after the big defeat at Barrow in 1978 a much changed Cumbrian team took on Lancashire at Whitehaven. Peter had done enough against the Australians to retain his place and he was joined in the second-row by his brother as the Gorleys played together at county level for the first time. This time the team was successful, winning 16-15, and the match began a personal sequence for Peter of five consecutive wins in county fixtures.

His next appearance came in September 1980, and a glance at the team sheet confirms the changing times at Derwent Park. Although the Gorleys, Eddie Bowman and Boxer Walker all kept their places, none of them was still at Workington. Having suddenly lost players of this calibre, Town's decline was very understandable.

The 1980-81 County Championship was a wonderful tournament for the Cumbrians who won their first championship since 1966 when they were known - properly, some would say - as Cumberland. After a win against Lancashire at Barrow in which Cumbria clawed back a nine-point deficit to win 19-16, the following fixture was another Wednesday night game two weeks later at Hull Kingston Rovers against Yorkshire. Peter recalls how some of the lesser known players raised their game and the result was 15 players totally committed to the cause. "With belief, you're half way there," said Peter. Very true - and a good maxim for life in general.

The *Rothman's Yearbook*, the game's 'bible' at the time, wrote: "For Cumbria, the Gorley brothers again stood out in a workmanlike pack..." Indeed, Peter scored his second try for Cumbria in a game even closer than the Lancashire fixture which the visitors won 17-16. The other try scorers were Boxer and lively hooker Alan McCurrie. Obviously the Cumbrians were happy to play on grounds called Craven Park.

After two games, both won, the title had been sealed and Lancashire and Yorkshire would be playing only for pride and to avoid the wooden spoon. It was therefore disappointing to discover that the County Championship trophy had not been taken to Craven

Park that evening. It seemed as though nobody in a position of authority really expected the Cumbrian team to win.

It was a long trip home but the team had won the County Championship, trophy on board or not. Peter remembers arriving home in the small hours but, fortunately, he had booked the following day off work. He and Les spent the day basking in the glory at the Loweswater Show where they watched rural Cumbrian pursuits such as hound trailing and fell running and drank Jennings Brothers' finest ale in the beautiful West Cumbrian countryside.

What made the victory even better was the fact that the tournament had been used as a test trial for the forthcoming series against New Zealand and on the strength of their good form the Gorley brothers, Arnie Walker and adopted Cumbrian Chris Camilleri went on to make their test debuts.

In 1981 Cumbria had a title to defend and their first match was at Wigan on 16 September. Lancashire, featuring Peter's Saints team mates Peter Glynn, Steve Peters and Harry Pinner, came off the back of a defeat the previous week against Yorkshire at Castleford, but could not improve and Cumbria won 27-15 with both Gorley brothers on the scoresheet. "Oh brother, the champs march on" read the *Daily Express* headline and county president Kenny Shepherd added his praise, calling both brothers "outstanding". Peter scored the first try after eight minutes when Barrow's Mel Mason put him in to send Cumbria on the way. The game was staged during one of the periodic Rugby Football League's purges on scrum offences and by half time both the hookers, Nicky Kiss and Alan McCurrie, had been sent off.

The following week's meeting with Yorkshire at Whitehaven was therefore to be the decider. The team at Wigan had contained some rather unfamiliar names after withdrawals through injuries, but some of the more established Cumbrian players had returned to fitness by match day. There was talk of making changes to the team, but after senior players from the first game had made their feelings known - they felt the replacements who had done so well against Lancashire deserved a second chance - the team which lined up at the Recreation Ground showed only one change.

Again, the *Rothman's Yearbook* praised Peter's performance: "The Gorleys once again shone for Cumbria, well supported by props [Harold] Henney and Malcolm Flynn," as the forwards laid the platform for the 20-10 win. Yorkshire's team selection had been hampered by injury problems, but nothing could put a damper on the feeling of satisfaction as the Cumbrians retained the title.

Unfortunately the tournament was plagued by disappointing attendances and even the deciding game was watched by only 2,352 spectators, albeit in dreadful weather conditions. Even smaller crowds in the 1982 competition when Cumbria, Gorley-less, surrendered the title to Yorkshire, were a factor in the tournament being scrapped.

Peter played eight times for his county, winning on five occasions and scoring three tries. It was a good record, as befits a player of his ability.

Peter's form also merited the call to represent his country and he did so with distinction, representing both England and Great Britain on three occasions each.

There was a school of thought that still persists, which says the international selectors visited Cumbria too infrequently and that a player with one of these outpost or unfashionable clubs, however good he may be, had less chance of selection than his counterparts at bigger clubs.

Peter's first England call up came a little over four months after his move to St Helens. Of course he'd been playing very well for Saints, but had he been playing that much better - or, indeed, any better - than when he was at Workington?

The St Helens club was well represented in February 1980 when Peter made his England debut at Hull Kingston Rovers' Craven Park. With Peter, also making their debuts, were Harry Pinner and Neil Holding while facing him in the Welsh pack were club mates Mel James, Roy Mathias and Chris Seldon. Peter began his England career with a 26-9 win and played well enough to retain his place in the squad for the following month's trip to Narbonne for England's second match in the European Championship tournament.

This memorable expedition holds many vivid memories for Peter, and doubtlessly for the other members of the England party.

Narbonne, about 50 miles to the north of Perpignan in France's south-western corner was, according to Peter, a real ghost town. "It was like something from a Western film," he recalls. "The only thing missing was the tumbleweed blowing along the deserted streets."

But on the pitch there was nothing moribund about the French team's approach. They were, to say the least, lively. The match was highlighted by rough and robust play from the home team which Peter initially saw from his place on the substitutes' bench but, after Wakefield prop Keith Rayne was viciously kicked in the face and stretchered off, it was Peter's turn to join in the fray.

The volatile and highly partisan 20,000 crowd only served to heighten the tension. England were leading 4-2 thanks to a Steve Evans try and a drop goal by Alan Redfearn when controversy broke out. The French centre Jean-Marc Bourret broke through the English ranks, drew full-back George Fairbairn and put his winger, Sebastian Rodriguez in to score - or so he thought. Referee Billy Thompson disagreed and ruled it a forward pass.

The French supporters went wild, throwing beer cans and hurling abuse at the referee. The situation was out of hand. There was the potential for a full-scale riot.

Towards the end of the match Billy told the players that next time there was a scrum near the half-way line he would blow the full-time whistle and it would be every man for himself. If each player took responsibility for his own safety, they should all be able to reach the sanctuary of the dressing room without being pelted by too many beer cans. There had been no more scores, so England had won 4-2.

The situation outside the ground after the match was very ugly and the players were kept in the dressing room for about an hour until tensions subsided. The French players came to swap shirts much to the disgust of Rugby League International Committee Chairman Bill Oxley who felt an exchange of jerseys would be seen as condoning the appalling French behaviour on the pitch. Nevertheless Peter did swap with Joel Roosebrouck, the French loose-forward and, arguably, their best player at the time.

Eventually the players were allowed to leave, but with a police escort. It was really referee Thompson with whom the French fans wished to discuss the match, but he had been whisked away earlier.

Back in the hotel bar, the atmosphere improved and, with Peter and Steve Evans working as barmen, the players and press enjoyed a convivial evening.

The French press was less than complimentary about the referee's performance and the next day he found himself temporarily infamous. "I'm a celebrity, get me out of here," Billy must have thought.

Unfortunately, Billy was having problems locating his passport and the prospect of being left behind in France when he was recognisable through newspaper photographs was distinctly unpleasant. Panic set in. Fortunately he was able to persuade a customs official to let him through on the strength of the photographs which could also have been his undoing had he had to stay. Later, of course, his passport was found lurking in an inside jacket pocket.

There was a wait of nearly 18 months before Peter's final England cap, earned on a visit to Ninian Park, Cardiff on 8 November 1981. Accompanied by seven others who had survived the Narbonne adventure and, this time, brother Les who had a place on the bench, Peter featured in Ninian Park's first rugby league international. The Welsh team was liberally sprinkled with recent converts from rugby union who were now starring for Cardiff City, rugby league's 1981 attempt at expansion in Wales which, sadly, failed to go the distance.

Despite a spirited Welsh rally near the end, backed by a partisan crowd, English experience won the day. The half time deadlock was broken by Peter who took a pass from Jeff Grayshon shortly after the interval to score an unconverted try which gave his country a lead it would never relinquish even though England had to survive a spirited Welsh comeback having seemingly had the game won when 13 points ahead at 20-7. England were rather relieved to hear the final whistle as they eventually won 20-15.

Peter was thrilled to be named man-of-the-match for England (Steve Fenwick securing the Welsh award) by writer and rugby league fan Colin Welland. Afterwards, on the way home, a few of the players got off the coach at Walsall where Steve Evans was a student at the time to join him for a few drinks, despite the selectors

103

pointing out that anyone who did not complete the journey home would be jeopardising his chances of being selected for Great Britain in the tests against France the following month. Peter and some others took the risk but were left to hitch their way home up the M6 motorway the following day. Luckily, the threat of non-selection was not carried out.

This game brought down the curtain on his England career. He had played three, won three and scored one try; so he had certainly done himself great credit.

The pinnacle, though, was representing Great Britain. Playing for his or her country is the crowning glory for any player in any sport, and rugby league is no exception. Playing for England was a great honour, but not as great an honour in rugby league as playing for Great Britain.

As already mentioned, the 1980 County Championship acted as a test trial and, having caught the selectors' eyes, Peter was duly selected for the third test. He might have played earlier but for his serious ankle injury at the end of September which certainly cost him his place in the Cumbrian and St Helens teams which defeated the New Zealanders and, possibly, a place in the first two tests.

On 15 November at Leeds, Peter proudly pulled on a Great Britain jersey for the first time. It was an important match; the first test, at Wigan, had been drawn and the Kiwis had won at Bradford, so a British win was needed to square the series. Britain rang the changes after previous disappointments; Les Gorley departed the international scene although he would subsequently return and Peter was joined by Arnie Walker, another Cumbrian making a long- awaited and deserved first appearance. Boxer made his mark by topping the British tackle count that day and Mick Burke was another who made a good debut kicking two goals, one from the touchline, and generally looking very solid at the back. By contrast, missed goal-kicks were to cost the Kiwis dearly.

The new selections played their parts as Britain, thanks to two late tries from man-of-the-match Des Drummond - "pound for pound, the hardest player to tackle," according to Peter - won 10-2 and prevented the Kiwis from winning the series as New Zealand had done when they had last visited in 1971.

Great Britain: Mick Burke (Widnes); Des Drummond (Leigh), John Joyner (Castleford), Steve Evans (Featherstone), John Atkinson (Leeds); John Woods (Leigh), Arnie Walker (Whitehaven); Trevor Skerrett (Hull), Keith Elwell (Widnes), Len Casey (Hull Kingston Rovers), Mick Adams (Widnes), Peter Gorley (St Helens), Steve Norton (Hull).

Subs: Ken Kelly (Warrington), Roy Holdstock (Hull Kingston Rovers)

New Zealand: Michael O'Donnell; Gary Prohm, John Whittaker, Bruce Dickison, Dane O'Hara; Fred Ah Kuoi, Gordon Smith; Mark Broadhurst, Alan Rushton, Kevin Tamati, Graeme West, Barry Edkins, Mark Graham.

Subs: Kevin Fisher, Howie Tamati.

Billy Thompson refereed the match which was watched by 8,210 supporters.

Peter eagerly awaited his next chance to represent his country, which would require him to continue his consistently fine club form.

Great Britain didn't play again for nearly 13 months during which time Peter had maintained his excellent form for St Helens, helped Cumbria regain their County Championship title and won the man-of-the-match award for England at Cardiff, so his selection in the team to play France on 6 December 1981 at Hull was not unexpected.

Les joined him in the second-row - they had finished the match at Cardiff as second-row partners and they were now to start that way for Great Britain. Under the headline "Brothers make rugby history" the *Workington Times & Star* carried an article on their selection which said: "that's the first time in living memory that such a momentous family double has taken place." Under a photograph of Peter and Les holding an international jersey and proudly sporting their international caps, Peter is quoted as saying: "I didn't know about it officially beforehand until I saw it in the papers. I'm bound to feel chuffed about it and I know Les is too."

The choice of The Boulevard, a French name, as the venue may have been designed to make the French feel at home but it was more likely to have been chosen to guarantee a good crowd. Hull was – and still is - a real hotbed of rugby league and more than 13,000 fans saw Great Britain win 37-0. The forwards laid the platform, but the match-winners were in the backs: wingers Des

Drummond with two tries and Henderson Gill - with a hat-trick - sharing five tries in a spectacular display of open rugby. It was the first time two British wingers had shared so many tries in a match.

The other British tries were scored by pacy inside backs Steve Hartley and John Woods who also kicked seven goals to add to one by George Fairbairn.

Great Britain: George Fairbairn (Hull KR); Des Drummond (Leigh), Mike Smith (Hull KR), John Woods (Leigh), Henderson Gill (Wigan); Steve Hartley (Hull KR) Andy Gregory (Widnes); Jeff Grayshon (Bradford N) David Ward (Leeds), Trevor Skerrett (Hull), Les Gorley (Widnes), Peter Gorley (St Helens), Steve Norton (Hull).

Subs: Mick Burke (Widnes), Eddie Szymala (Barrow).

France: Marcel Pillon; Sebastian Rodriguez, Serge Costals, Hugues Ratier, Laurent Girardet; Eric Walligunda, Christian Scicchitano; Henri Daniel, Christian Maccali, Dominique Verdiere, Jose Gine, Marc Ambert, Joel Roosebrouck.

Subs: Michel Laville, Thierry Barnabe.

The return match took place two weeks later in Marseille and Peter recalls one of the more memorable events surrounding the trip. After a midnight arrival, Les, Peter, Steve Norton and Trevor Skerrett found a 24-hour bar where they relaxed and chatted into the small hours. However, some of the locals were a little less than friendly. When an Alsatian dog broke free from behind the bar and nobody restrained it, Les struck it on the head with an ashtray which angered the locals and unfortunately Les was sprayed in the face with table cleaner

The locals must have been a tough bunch to even consider confronting the quartet of Messrs Gorley, Gorley, Norton and Skerrett. Marseille certainly has a tough reputation, but Peter recalled: "It's actually quite pleasant round the harbour".

On the pitch the story was very different from two weeks previously. Eddie Szymala, Barrow's tough forward, took Peter's second-row place while Peter was dropped to the bench. Naturally, there were few changes in the British line up whereas the French made wholesale alterations in their team.

The match took place at a football ground, a little away from the traditional rugby league area, and 6,500 spectators gathered hoping to see a French improvement. They were not disappointed. The game was a complete contrast to the previous encounter as this time the French played with the flair and speed that the British had demonstrated in Hull and they stormed to a 19-2 victory.

Unfortunately, the match had much in common with the Narbonne experience, violence and foul play being to the fore. It was a stormy affair from the start. The first half was punctuated by frequent niggles and the British players were never allowed to repeat the flowing, three-quarter dominated play which had been seen a fortnight previously. The bad tempers boiled over just before half time when Les Gorley was sent off after flattening one of the French second-rowers. The Australian referee Greg Hartley, appointed after continual calls for neutral officials in internationals and who had also officiated in the first match at Hull, extended the interval to give the players time to cool down and to explain that he would stop the match altogether if players' behaviour did not improve. "That's not a match, that's war," he said, but didn't carry out his threat to abandon the match and play did continue.

Peter played the last 12 minutes as a substitute for Eddie Szymala, but his arrival was too late to influence the result. It was not France's highest score against Great Britain, but the 17-point margin was the greatest so far in the cross-channel fixtures.

Great Britain: Mick Burke (Widnes); Des Drummond (Leigh), Mike Smith (Hull KR), John Woods (Leigh), Henderson Gill (Wigan); Steve Hartley (Hull KR), Andy Gregory (Widnes); Jeff Grayshon (Bradford N), David Watkinson (Hull KR), Trevor Skerrett (Hull), Les Gorley (Widnes), Eddie Szymala (Barrow), Steve Norton (Hull).

Subs: George Fairbairn (Hull KR), Peter Gorley (St Helens)

France: Andre Perez; Patrick Solal, Jacques Guiges, Guy Delaunay, Sebastian Rodriguez; Michel Laville, Christian Scicchitano; Charles Zalduendo, Christian Maccali, Jose Gine, Guy Lafforgue, Marc Ambert, Joel Roosebrouck.

Subs: Etienne Kaminski, Thierry Barnabe

The French tries were scored by Solal with two, Kaminski and Scicchitano. Perez kicked three goals and Laville dropped a goal. A solitary goal by Woods was all the British had to show for their efforts.

More than half the team, Peter included, failed to feature in the next test, a mauling the following October by the all-conquering Australians, and, indeed, Peter was not selected to play for his country again. He was 31 years old and the selectors had decided to bring in younger men. However, the younger men had a chastening experience in the autumn of 1982 from which British international rugby league has, arguably, still not recovered.

Because of his late entry to the professional ranks, Peter was 29 when he made his British debut. On how many more occasions would he have represented his country had he left the amateur game earlier?

15. *This is your life*

Peter had struck up a firm friendship with Mal Meninga during his stay at Saints and although he didn't know it at the time, this would lead to the trip of a lifetime nearly a decade later in August 1994.

Peter was in the supermarket next to Workington Town's ground (it had actually been built on the training ground that the club used during Peter's time) when he bumped into Keith Ray who sold match tickets at the Workington club. Keith told Peter that Richard Farmer had phoned from Australia, anxious to contact him.

Richard phoned again with some excellent news. A *This is your life* presentation was being staged for Mal Meninga and Peter had been selected for a 'wild card' appearance. How was he fixed for a flight Down Under in three days' time?

At the end of the same week Peter found himself on a long and complicated journey. Having made his way to Manchester Airport he flew via Heathrow and Sydney to Canberra where he was allowed some rest in a hotel. He then moved to Brisbane where he stayed with Peter McIlwaine, a good friend of Mal who had been best man at his wedding.

Ten years on, Peter can recall events during his nine-day stay as if they happened yesterday. "What a fantastic trip it was," he said. "People there were wonderful - they couldn't do enough to make sure that I enjoyed myself."

He enjoyed his stay at his host's house but one hairy moment sticks in his mind. Mal's friend was an undercover policeman who as a matter of course was armed as Peter discovered when he first put his bag in the car boot and spotted the gun, although it was explained that the only time Peter McIlwaine had had to use it was when McIlwaine had accidentally run over a koala bear which needed to be put out if its misery. However, one morning, at breakfast, Peter was shown five bullet holes in a Land Rover parked near his bedroom window and he realised that he had had something of a lucky escape.

Peter McIlwaine had been on an undercover operation in the bush staking out a drugs gang and it seemed that one of them had returned during the night to put the frighteners on him although he had picked the wrong vehicle - the Land Rover belonged to a neighbour.

Aside from this excitement, Peter was able to relax in Queensland and he visited the Gold Coast and Surfers' Paradise where it was warm enough to go swimming in the sea, even in an Australian winter, quite unlike the beach at Allonby up the road from Broughton in a Cumbrian winter.

Eventually Peter took the plane to Melbourne where Mal and he met up with other great Australian rugby league players such as Ricky Stuart, Alfie Langer and Laurie Daley and he recalls a meal in a Thai restaurant - one of Melbourne's finest - which had been specially opened for Mal's party. There was a large choice of exotic and unusual food such as crocodile and kangaroo, but Peter, sticking with what he knew, chose the chicken. On another occasion they ate Mexican food in a casino - on the house - and the champagne flowed freely on the plane journeys. Wherever he went, Mal was afforded film star status - treatment akin to that afforded top Premiership footballers - which, given that he was a superstar in his country's number one winter spectator sport, was not surprising.

Nerves were jangling on the night of the presentation - it isn't easy standing and talking in front of people when you are not used to it and, when the television cameras are present, then it must be doubly nerve-wracking. Peter was second on stage which meant he didn't have to wait too long for his appearance and he was welcomed by master of ceremonies Shaun McRae who later coached St Helens and then Hull. Mal feigned surprise and pretended not to know who Peter was which spiced up the occasion for the English visitor.

"But the best thing really," Peter reminded me, "was that everybody pushed the boat out for me." Later Peter McIlwaine took Peter to the Australian parliament and to Sydney Harbour with its opera house and famous bridge, similar to Widnes and Runcorn. And finally, he was taken to Sydney's most famous surfing beach, Bondi. It was the trip of a lifetime, to places that many people can only dream about, but was a suitable reward for the valued and appreciated hospitality and friendship that Peter had shown towards Mal when the latter was a stranger a long way from home.

Peter supporting Mal Meninga for St Helens at Knowsley Road
(Photo: Courtesy Alex Service)

Peter with Harry Pinner and Chris Arkwright at Harry Pinner's pub, the Parr Arms, at Grappenhall near Warrington.
(Photo: Peter Cropper)

Harry Pinner was a ball handler supreme, tenacious tackler, regular try scorer, place kicker of repute, drop goal king (no one else is anywhere near his total of 'one-pointers' for the Saints) - Harry could do the lot. He played 342 times for the Saints between 1975 and 1986 and scored over 600 points for the club. He was without doubt the linchpin of the St Helens team, and he went on to captain the club with distinction. While at Knowsley Road, he appeared six times for Great Britain, which, in the opinion of many experts, was far too infrequently, even allowing for the glut of quality loose-forwards at the time. Truly a great player who would have been a real sensation in a top quality team, which, unfortunately for much of his career St Helens could not boast.

Chris Arkwright was one of Peter's contemporaries at Knowsley Road and one of the toughest and most committed players to play for St Helens. He played 271 games for the club, registering 90 tries, he captained the team at Wembley in 1987 and he represented Lancashire, England and Great Britain. He could play centre, stand-off and loose-forward with equal skill.

112

16. A working man from Workington

In the beginning, back in the nineteenth century, rugby football was an amateur game.

The professional branch of the game - rugby league, then called Northern Union - came into being in 1895 when workers in the industrial north demanded 'broken time' payment because playing on a Saturday, then the traditional playing day, was costing them money in lost wages. Additionally, many northern clubs wanted to hold cup and league matches. The governing body, the Rugby Football Union, refused to countenance the approach of the northern clubs, and so the great game of rugby league was born at a meeting in the George Hotel, a handsome building situated in Huddersfield town centre.

One hundred years later, the 1990s saw the advent of Super League and full-time professionalism for the top clubs. No longer did players in the higher echelons of the game have to combine playing and training with employment elsewhere as Peter and his team mates did. Top players today are fully focused on the game. In Peter's era they had other fish to fry.

Steel production and mining for coal - or iron ore in the case of the Florence Mine at Egremont - were the main employers in West Cumbria. The Corus plant at Workington, large now, used to be even bigger and employed many men. One of many mines in the area, the Haig pit above Whitehaven, where enthusiasts are now building up a very interesting museum, had coal seams which stretched many miles under the sea. As a display in the museum indicates, there has always been a very strong link between rugby and mining - how many times did we hear television commentator Eddie Waring's story of clubs in mining communities calling down the pit shaft when they wanted a new prop or scrum-half? And two of Peter's best friends, Arnie Walker and Eddie Bowman, who were employed at the mine, are pictured at the museum to show this link.

Peter worked full-time too, and when his travelling to training and matches at St Helens is taken into consideration, it is amazing how he found the stamina to keep going.

When he first played professionally, Peter was employed as a drayman at Jennings brewery. He enjoyed the work for two main reasons. Firstly, it enabled him to see many fine parts of Cumbria which he might not otherwise have seen. Every day was different. His work might take him to Keswick, on to Penrith and then further into the less well-known and underrated Eden Valley. The next day might see him visiting the pubs in the beautiful Buttermere Valley or heading out to the coast. Secondly, the work helped maintain his fitness levels as handling beer barrels helped build up the strength and stamina so vital for a rugby forward. It also brought him the 15 minutes of fame which Andy Warhol had promised everyone when Border Television filmed him at the Steam Packet in Workington and other Jennings pubs in Keswick ahead of his victorious Lancashire Cup Final appearance in 1977.

He later worked in open cast mining which was quite prevalent in the coastal area. Although better paid, the work was not as enjoyable because it was tedious and repetitive. The days were long, muddy and dusty, and lacked the variety of his previous job.

Now he is based at the nuclear reprocessing plant at Sellafield where he has done various jobs. Peter is happy to work there despite traffic problems at both ends of the working day. The road from Cockermouth to Egremont and then down the coast to the plant is always busy and it is necessary to leave home very early to avoid the congestion. The end of the working day also offers similar difficulties.

In his days with Saints there was perhaps a chance to grab a sandwich and a quick drink before he had to hit the road to attend training. It was a long drive, usually two-and-a-half hours, which, provided it wasn't raining and the car wasn't being continually drenched by the spray from articulated lorries, he was usually able to enjoy with some music on the car stereo to keep him company. At Saints he trained once a week at Knowsley Road and once a week at home and obviously every game, home or away, apart from the occasional fixture at Workington or Whitehaven, involved a long journey.

Travelling has left him with many memories. He recalls an episode when he was driving a hire car with which he was unfamiliar. The car had fog lights which he was unable to switch off

114

and, inevitably, Peter was stopped by a policeman who happened to be a Wigan supporter. The officer said he had no alternative but to book Peter because he was a Saint; had he been a Wigan player he would have let him off. He was joking - after all, some people would claim a sense of humour is essential to watch Wigan.

One Thursday, after a midweek match on the Tuesday, Peter arrived for training only to discover that coach Billy Benyon had decided that a soak in the bath would be more beneficial than a strenuous training session. "I've come all this way for a bath!" said Peter. "We're not so far behind in Cumbria that we don't have baths, you know."

The journeys were long but a lengthy trip, when undertaken frequently and it becomes routine, does seem to shorten. Peter also had two favourite stopping off points - the Eagle and Child at Staveley, near Kendal, and the King's Head at Thirlspot, near Keswick - and he became friendly with the staff in those establishments. Often he would meet Les, another long distance rugby commuter, who would be on his way back from training at Widnes and the Gorleys would compare notes for a while before resuming their journeys.

There's little doubt that players today have it considerably easier than Peter did in respect of training and travelling but he gives the impression that he enjoyed his time so much and has so many good memories that he probably would not have had it any other way.

No regrets!

In 2000, the villagers of Broughton built a mosaic to mark the Millennium
and the village's achievements. Above is part of the mosaic, below the
section that shows the Rugby Caps including Peter and Les Gorley
(Photos: Peter Cropper)

17. Today's Cumbrian man

These days Peter has no direct involvement with the game. Of course, he chose not to leave Great Broughton even when he played for St Helens and he still lives in the village just off the main street. From his house he enjoys a wonderful view across fields to the River Derwent as it meanders towards the coast entering the Irish Sea - appropriately - at Derwent Park. Beyond this scene, the fells of the north-western corner of the Lake District rear up impressively with the great fell of Grasmoor prominent.

Although maligned in some quarters and regarded by some as 'the land time forgot', West Cumbria offers much and Peter easily fills his free time, enjoying the fresh air and sometimes walking in the fells. He keeps himself in shape with regular visits to the well-appointed Ted's Gym in Workington, so fitness is no problem and he can meet the challenges posed by the Cumbrian mountains.

He doesn't watch much live sport these days, but is occasionally persuaded to go to Derwent Park to see a match and in February 2003, Peter went to watch Workington play Barrow in the Arriva Trains Cup. It was the week after Workington's embarrassing Challenge Cup defeat against local amateurs Wath Brow and morale was low. Added to that was a bitter wind blowing in from the Solway carrying heavy snow showers and it was not surprising that there was a disappointing attendance. Just 578 hardy souls turned out for the repeat of the 1955 Challenge Cup Final - how both clubs must wish they could turn the clock back 50 years.

For the record, 48 years later Barrow won 20-10. Workington held territorial advantage for much of the game but Barrow's tackling held the home team at bay. The contrast between the present day and Peter's time with Town was painfully obvious and, as Peter rightly observed, the Workington club is trapped in something of a vicious circle. Not much will attract promising youngsters to join the club. There are insufficient funds to buy players, and the current crop, despite its enthusiasm, is not good enough to take Town forward. Supporters feel disinclined to return, but without support the money required to invest in new players is not forthcoming... it's a sadly familiar story, not unique to Workington Town.

The atmosphere in the players' bar afterwards was rather subdued, most of the people there being able to recall better days. As the man-of-the-match sponsor, Ted Clifton of Ted's Gym, observed: "It's a great shame. There's great potential in this town. If there were a good Super League team at Derwent Park there would be crowds of 8,000 people."

Many fans would agree with him. West Cumbria, with its strong amateur game, is still a hot bed of rugby league. But "Who's going to watch that?" was the general feeling after the match.

Peter, in common with many former players, does not believe that the quality of today's game is as high as when he played. Fitness levels are higher now, but are the flair players missing? Where are the really crafty little scrum-halves and the really clever loose-forwards with their subtle skills? In the 21st century, the game seems to be based on power. Certainly there is a problem from the point of view of strong competition, but this issue is certainly not restricted to the sport of rugby league. There seems to be little chance of building a team, entering the elite and breaking the stranglehold which certain teams have on the trophies. A little over 25 years on from Workington's Lancashire Cup triumph, it is difficult to envisage Workington ever beating Wigan again in a final. Indeed, it is even hard to imagine when they might next even play against each other outside an occasional Challenge Cup meeting.

A big difference between Peter's era and today is summer rugby, although sitting at a cold Derwent Park in February it was hard to believe. Peter feels playing in summer is good for the spectator as bad weather keeps a lot of people away but, conversely, summer provides a number of distractions such as gardening, cricket, trips to the coast and expeditions into the Cumbrian hills. These activities can mean that the rugby league terraces are sparsely populated.

Some Cumbrians are also attracted to typically local pursuits not particularly followed elsewhere. Hound trailing, a local activity, is not something which has appealed to Peter - it is a preference of his brother - but, thanks to Les, Peter has enjoyed the challenges of Cumberland wrestling.

The Gorley brothers attended the Langholm Show over the Scottish border one year. It was an early start and later on, after a few drinks, Peter discovered that Les had entered him for the Cumberland wrestling competition. Peter was pitted against Roger Grant from Boroughmuir and in the rain he took on his more experienced opponent. He was one fall down, but giving a good account of himself, when he was injured during the second fall by, according to one veteran attender: "the best throw I've ever seen in all my years of coming to this show."

Peter was later misquoted in a report of the Show as saying: "it's a lot harder than rugby league", and he was none-too-pleased when he read this. Rugby league has had its share of bad press over the years.

These days the knees which have taken a battering from so much rugby might object to such punishment. Conquering such peaks as Great Gable is more suitable exercise.

For more leisurely indoor pursuits Peter crosses the river to Brigham to enjoy his weekly game of darts in the local league and occasionally he airs his general knowledge in quizzes at the Bitter End pub in Cockermouth. But more than anything, he enjoys the quiet life, close to his roots. He talks enthusiastically of the annual village carnival and sits comfortably in the Punch Bowl and other watering holes in the village.

Visitors to Broughton can see an impressive mosaic which was designed to commemorate the new millennium and, on one section, the names of those men from the village who have won international rugby caps can be seen. Peter's name is there, of course, together with that of his brother, Roland Rogers, John Graham and all-time great, the late Brian Edgar.

But success has never changed Peter. His modesty ensures that.

Halifax versus St Helens 17 March 1985. The result was 19-19.
(Photo: Courtesy Alex Service)

18. Peter's party

Peter celebrated his half century in July 2001, and the occasion was celebrated in style in and around Great Broughton.

The look on Peter's face as he entered the Legion club on Saturday 7 July at Great Broughton was priceless, and worth all the hard work and careful planning.

I had received a call a few weeks earlier inviting me and my wife Josephine to attend a surprise party in honour of Peter's 50th birthday. I was delighted to be asked, and we began to look forward to another weekend in one of our favourite parts of the world. At about the same time Steve Clarke telephoned from Workington. He had heard of my plans to write a book about Peter and asked if I could present a St Helens rugby league jersey to Peter and say a few words after a veterans' rugby union match on the Sunday afternoon. Again I was delighted, and accepted with some trepidation, realising what a daunting prospect this could be.

As the weekend approached, I spent time carefully researching and preparing the speech. I managed to remain focussed and produced a speech which would, I hoped, be well received by the rugby playing fraternity of West Cumbria.

According to our instructions, we were to be at the Legion club for 7.30pm on Saturday so that everyone could be settled in for Peter's arrival. Some of his former team mates were already there, and it was interesting to be in the same room as such players as Boxer Walker, Eddie Bowman, Peter's brother Les and Smiler Allen. Also present were Harry Beverley, less recognisable without the beard he used to sport when playing for Dewsbury, Workington and Fulham, and Tony Scott, survivor of Carlisle's horrendous 112-0 Lancashire Cup defeat at St Helens in 1986.

Peter had been deliberately distracted during the day by a cycle ride to the coast with his son while the preparations for his party were carried out. He was under the impression that his evening appointment at the Legion was for a photo call, and this is why his surprise was so genuine when he walked through the door. "I thought I was gate-crashing someone else's party," he said later. "It was only when I recognised so many familiar faces that I realised it was for me."

A modest man, Peter was clearly touched by the whole affair and it was very evident that he enjoyed himself. He was clearly unperturbed when given the microphone and asked to speak nor did he seem concerned by the enthusiastic requests to do a dance routine with one of his old friends which he performed with great aplomb. The number of people who crammed into the club that night reflected the admiration, affection and respect which Peter has earned in the small village and beyond. Clearly everyone enjoyed the atmosphere and the opportunity to reminisce and socialise with old friends, and everyone's tastes were catered for by a tremendous buffet which had been prepared with great skill and dedication during Peter's absence that afternoon. The centrepiece of the magnificent spread was a wonderful cake decorated in the red and white colours which Peter had worn with great distinction on so many occasions while at Knowsley Road.

The almost tropical heat of the Saturday evening had been replaced by weather more typical of the region when Sunday morning dawned, but perhaps the drizzle which was falling was more suitable for a veterans' rugby match than the previous day's stifling conditions.

We accepted the kind invitation from the previous evening and took morning coffee in Peter's conservatory. Unfortunately the misty and drizzly conditions meant that the views towards the mountains could only be imagined and not enjoyed. Looking particularly spruce and still in shape, Peter picked up his bag and announced he was setting off to Cockermouth Rugby Union club.

"Summer rugby," said one of the spectators ironically as the rain started to fall more heavily at kick-off. Cockermouth Rugby Union club has a favourable location on the south side of town next to the Buttermere road, and on a good day there would be fine views similar to those from Great Broughton. Unfortunately, these were also left to the imagination.

The match itself was played in tremendous spirit with great commitment and skill as the players fought off the two problems - wet conditions underfoot and the relentless march of Father Time. It was strange to see Peter operating in the backs having spent all his professional career in the pack, but he showed his old handling, running and tackling expertise before being forced to retire with a knee injury. An entertaining, free-scoring and inevitably sportingly contested match which featured lots of enterprising running - the players had agreed to dispense with the kicking game so often associated with rugby union - was brought to a close. Peter received the sincere congratulations and best wishes of all the participants, and the very wet players and spectators retreated to the dry comfort of the clubhouse.

There was clearly no rush to start the speeches, as post-match celebrations began and the drinks started to flow.

Eventually, a very tasty curry was produced and enjoyed before the big moment arrived. Mitch, the youngest of the three Gorley brothers, was to introduce me, and then the floor would be mine.

Confronted with a sea of faces, I began the carefully prepared speech. It soon became apparent that I needed have no fear of addressing a crowd of strangers who listened attentively and with interest to the rugby league fan's perspective of Peter's career. I survived, despite a little gentle barracking from Les, who of course played for Widnes when they often held the upper hand against the Saints. At the end Peter was clearly delighted with both the Saints shirt which had "GORLEY 50" emblazoned across the back and the Workington Town rugby league shirt he received from his Mum.

Suitably lubricated, the various performers were now in a position to began their post-match entertainment. With John Cusack, chairman of the rugby club, outstanding in the role of master of ceremonies, the early evening proceedings were guaranteed to be a huge success. Clearly prepared for this, many people seemed to have something up their sleeve - a song, a poem or perhaps even 'stand up comedy' all rendered in the individual's inimitable style. After more than an hour of excellent entertainment for which a charge could justifiably have been levied, so high was the standard, a spoof *This is Your Life*, superbly prepared and brilliantly acted out by some of Peter's friends, provided a final surprise to what had been, in Peter's own words, "The best weekend of my life."

Appendix: Statistics and records

By Robert Gate and Peter Lush.

	Appearances	Tries
Workington Town		
Debut: 2 November 1975 versus Blackpool Borough (away)		
1975-76	15 + 4	2
1976-77	33 + 5	4
1977-78	38	6
1978-79	29	1

St Helens
Debut: 9 October 1979 versus Rochdale Hornets (home) BBC2 Floodlit Trophy first round

1979-80	31	5
1980-81	29 + 2	9
1981-82	29 + 1	11
1982-83	35 + 2	9
1983-84	37 + 3	4
1984-85	41	8
1985-86	23 + 1	0

Whitehaven
Debut: 28 March 1986 versus Workington Town (away)

1985-86	1	0
1986-87	2	0

Career Totals:

	Appearances	Tries
Workington Town	115 + 9	13
St Helens	225 + 9	46
Whitehaven	3	0
Cumbria	8	3
England	2 + 1	1
Great Britain	2 + 1	0
Grand Total	355 + 20	63

Peter Gorley's international appearances

Great Britain

1980-81

New Zealand at Headingley 15 November 1980. Won 10-2.
Great Britain: M. Burke, D. Drummond, J. Joyner, S. Evans, J. Atkinson,
J. Woods, A. Walker, T. Skerrett, K. Elwell, L. Casey, P. Gorley, M. Adams, S.
Norton.
Subs: K. Kelly, R. Holdstock
New Zealand: M. O'Donnell, G. Prohm, J. Whittaker, B. Dickison,
D. O'Hara, F. Ah Kuoi, G. Smith, M. Broadhurst, A. Rushton, K. Tamati,
G. West, B. Edkins, M. Graham.
Subs: K. Fisher, H. Tamati

1981-82:

France at Hull 6 December 1981. Won 37-0.
Great Britain: G. Fairbairn, D. Drummond, M. Smith, J. Woods, H. Gill,
S. Hartley, A. Gregory, J. Grayshon, D. Ward, T. Skerrett, L. Gorley,
P. Gorley, S. Norton. Subs: M. Burke, E. Syzmala.
France: M. Pillon, S. Rodriguez, S. Costals, H. Ratier, L. Giradet,
E. Walligunda, C. Scicchitano, H. Daniel, C. Maccali, D. Verdiere, J. Gine, M.
Ambert, J. Roosebrouck.
Subs: M. Laville, T. Barnabe.

France at Marseilles 20 December 1981. Lost 19-2.
Great Britain: M. Burke, D. Drummond, M. Smith, J. Woods, H. Gill, Hartley,
A. Gregory, J. Grayshon, Watkinson, Skerrett, L. Gorley,
E. Syzmala, S. Norton. Sub: P. Gorley
France: A. Perez, P. Solai, J. Guigues, G. Delaunay, S. Rodriguez,
M. Laville, C. Scicchitano, C. Zalduendo, C. Maccali, J. Gine, G. Lafforgue, M.
Ambert, J. Roosebrouck.
Subs: E. Kaminski, T. Barnabe.

England:

1979-80

Wales at Hull KR 29 February 1980. Won 26-9.
(European Championship)
England: G. Fairbairn, S. Wright, J. Joyner, M. Smith, D. Drummond, S. Evans, N. Holding, R. Holdstock, D. Ward, Keith Rayne, L. Casey, P. Gorley, H. Pinner.
Subs: J. Woods, J. Grayshon.
Wales: H. Box, B. Juliff, G. Walters, B. Francis, P. Prendiville, P. Woods, N. Flowers, M. James, D. Parry, G. Shaw, C. Seldon, J. Bevan, R. Mathias.
Subs: S. Diamond, M. McJennett.

France at Narbonne 16 March 1980. Won 4-2.
(European Championship)
England: G. Fairbairn, D. Drummond, M. Smith, J. Joyner, S. Evans, J. Woods, A. Redfearn, R. Holdstock, D. Ward, Keith Rayne, J. Grayshon, P. Smith, H. Pinner.
Subs: P. Glynn, P. Gorley.
France: F. Tranier, J-M. Gonzales, C. Laumond, J-M. Bourret, S. Rodriguez, M. Mazare, Y. Greseque, M. Chantal, H. Daniel, D. Hermet, C. Baile, J. Gine, J. Roosebrouck.
Subs: C. Maccali, J. Guigue

1981-82

Wales at Cardiff 8 November 1981. Won 20-15
England: G. Fairbairn, D. Drummond, M. Smith, L. Dyl, H. Gill, J. Woods, S. Nash, J. Grayshon, D. Ward, J. Millington, P. Lowe, P. Gorley, S. Norton.
Subs: S. Evans, L. Gorley
Wales: G. Pritchard, A. Cambriani, S. Bayliss, S. Fenwick, J. Bevan, D. Wilson, N. Flowers, M. James, D. Parry, T. David, M. Herdman, G. Shaw, P. Ringer.
Subs: P. Prendiville, R. Owen

Peter Gorley's Cumbria appearances

5 October 1977 Yorkshire 28 Cumbria 10 at York

P. Charlton (Workington Town): R. McConnell (Barrow), R. Wilkins (Workington Town), J. Risman (Workington Town), D. Collister (Workington Town); M. Mason (Barrow), F. Jones (Barrow); H. McCourt (Barrow), A. McCurrie (Whitehaven), E. Bowman (Workington Town), P. Gorley (Workington Town), T. Gainford (Whitehaven), P. Hogan (Barrow).
Sub: G. Cottier (Whitehaven).
Tries: Gorley, Cottier.
Goals: Hogan 2.
Crowd: 2,633

1 October 1978   Cumbria 4 Australians 47 at Barrow

P. Charlton (Workington Town); J. Risman (Workington Town), J. Stewart (Whitehaven), R. Wilkins (Workington Town), I. MacCorquodale (Workington Town); R. McConnell (Barrow), A. Walker (Workington Town); S. Hogan (Barrow), A. McCurrie (Wakefield Trinity), E. Bowman (Workington Town), P. Gorley (Workington Town), P. Cavanagh (Barrow), P. Hogan (Barrow).
Subs: T. Thompson (Barrow), A. Banks (Workington Town).
Goals: MacCorquodale 2
Crowd: 5,946

11 October 1978 Cumbria 16 Lancashire 15 at Whitehaven

P. Charlton (Workington Town); M. McMullen (Whitehaven), J. Stewart (Whitehaven), G. Pritchard (Barrow), I. MacCorquodale (Workington Town); D. McMillan (Workington Town), A. Walker (Workington Town); J. Hamilton (Blackpool Borough), A. McCurrie (Wakefield Trinity), E. Bowman (Workington Town), P. Gorley (Workington Town), L. Gorley (Workington Town), T. Gainford (Whitehaven).
Tries: Walker, McCurrie.
Goals: MacCorquodale 5.
Crowd: 2,500

3 September 1980 Cumbria 19 Lancashire 16 at Barrow

T. Thompson (Whitehaven); K. Hodgson (Whitehaven), P. Stoddart (Whitehaven), I. Ball (Barrow), C. Camilleri (Barrow); I. Rudd (Workington Town), A. Walker (Whitehaven); R. Calvin (Whitehaven), A. McCurrie (Wakefield Trinity), J. Cunningham (Workington Town), V. Fox (Whitehaven), L. Gorley (Widnes), P. Gorley (St Helens).
Subs: E. Bowman (Leigh), M. Mason (Barrow).
Tries: Fox, Rudd, Ball.
Goals: Ball 5.
Crowd: 1,700

127

17 September 1980 Yorkshire 16 Cumbria 17 at Hull KR

S. Tickle (Barrow); J. Bulman (Whitehaven), P. Stoddart (Whitehaven), I. Ball (Barrow), C. Camilleri (Barrow): I. Rudd (Workington Town), A. Walker (Whitehaven); E. Bowman (Leigh), A. McCurrie (Wakefield Trinity), J. Cunningham (Workington Town), V. Fox (Whitehaven), L. Gorley (Widnes), P. Gorley (St. Helens).
Subs: M. Mason (Barrow), M. Flynn (Barrow).
Tries: Walker, P. Gorley, McCurrie.
Goals: Ball 3.
Drop goals: Ball, Cunningham.
Crowd: 2,815

16 September 1981 Lancashire 15 Cumbria 27 at Wigan

S. Tickle (Barrow); R. McConnell (Barrow), P. Stoddart (Whitehaven), J. Jones (Workington Town), D. Beck (Workington Town); M. Mason (Barrow), A. Walker (Whitehaven); H. Henney (Salford), A. McCurrie (Wakefield Trinity), M. Flynn (Barrow), L. Gorley (Widnes), P. Gorley (St Helens), G. Cottier (Whitehaven).
Subs: J. Stewart (Whitehaven), R. Blackwood (Workington Town).
Tries: Walker 2, McConnell, L. Gorley, P. Gorley.
Goals: Tickle 4, Stoddart, Walker.
Crowd: 1,106

23 September 1981 Cumbria 20 Yorkshire 10 at Whitehaven

L. Hopkins (Workington Town); R. McConnell (Barrow), P. Stoddart (Whitehaven), J. Jones (Workington Town), D. Beck (Workington Town); M. Mason (Barrow), A. Walker (Whitehaven); H. Henney (Salford), A. McCurrie (Wakefield Trinity), M. Flynn (Barrow), P. Gorley (St Helens), L. Gorley (Widnes), G. Cottier (Whitehaven).
Subs: J. Stewart (Whitehaven), R. Blackwood (Workington Town).
Tries: Flynn, Beck, Mason, Walker.
Goals: Hopkins 4.
Crowd: 2,353

9 November 1982 Cumbria 2 Australians 41 at Carlisle

L. Hopkins (Workington Town); R. Mackie (Whitehaven), R. McConnell (Barrow), D. Bell (Carlisle), T. Moore (Barrow); M. Mason (Barrow), D. Cairns (Barrow); S. Herbert (Barrow), A. McCurrie (Oldham), M. Flynn (Barrow), W. Pattinson (Workington Town), P. Gorley (St Helens), D. Hadley (Barrow).
Subs: D. Beck (Workington Town), I. Hartley (Workington Town).
Goal: Hopkins.
Crowd: 5,748

Peter Gorley's club record

	League	Cups (semi-final or better)
Workington Town		
1975-76	3rd (Second Division)	Lancashire Cup semi-final
1976-77	12th (First Division)	Lancashire Cup finalists
1977-78	11th (First Division)	Lancashire Cup winners
1978-79	9th (First Division)	Lancashire Cup finalists
St Helens		
1979-80	8th (First Division)	BBC2 Floodlit Trophy semi-final
1980-81	8th (First Division)	Challenge Cup semi-final Premiership semi-final
1981-82	7th (First Division)	Lancashire Cup semi-final
1982-83	4th (First Division)	Lancashire Cup finalists
1983-84	6th (First Division)	John Player Trophy semi-final Premiership semi-final
1984-85	2nd (First Division)	Lancashire Cup winners Premiership winners
1985-86	3rd (First Division)	Lancashire Cup semi-final John Player Trophy semi-final

Peter also played three games for Whitehaven at the end of his career.

130

A Dream Come True
A Rugby League Life
By Doug Laughton
with Andrew Quirke

Doug Laughton is one of the key figures in British Rugby League in the last 40 years.

His playing career started at St Helens in 1962. He then moved to Wigan and captained them in the 1970 Challenge Cup Final.

A further move followed to Widnes, with more success, including four Wembley finals.

He also captained Great Britain and was a member of the last British Lions team to beat the Australians.

As a coach, he won every trophy in the game with Widnes, including a memorable World Club Challenge victory over Canberra in 1989. He signed Jonathan Davies and Martin Offiah for Widnes. He managed Leeds from 1991 to 1995, which included two more Wembley finals.

This hard hitting book covers his full career and will be of interest to all Rugby League fans.

Published in October 2003 in hardback at £14.95.
Available from all good bookshops, (ISBN: 1903659124)
or post free from London League Publications Ltd, PO Box 10441, London E14 8WR.
Cheques to London League Publications Ltd.
Credit card orders via our website: www.llpshop.co.uk

Give it to Kelly!
A Rugby League Saga

By John D. Vose

Foreword by John Etty

John D. Vose's new book completes a trilogy about Bramfield Rovers, a fictional struggling Lancashire Rugby League side from the 1930s.

Following on from his previous books *Up t' Rovers* and *Put Ref. A Jersey On!*, this book recalls a more innocent time for the game, away from the modern day pressures of professional sport.

Readers will be entertained and bemused by:

- Club scout Stanley Keighley's scouting mission to a posh North Yorkshire Rugby Union club;
- A wizard centre with a double-barrelled name;
- A Russian spy masquerading as a belly dancer from Heckmondwike on the run from Captain Montague-Morency of MI6; and
- A light-fingered, smooth-talking Australian: a try-scoring rugby genius who can streak past defenders with the agility of a cheetah, beguile Lancashire barmaids and daughters of the aristocracy with equal aplomb, and then set the police forces of Yorkshire and Lancashire hot on his trail.

About the author: John D. Vose grew up in St Helens in the 1930s. He has written widely on many subjects as well as Rugby League. He now lives in Blackpool.

Published in September 2003 at £8.95. Special Offer – post only - for readers of this book £8.00 post free ISBN: 1903659-11-6

Order from: London League Publications Ltd, PO Box 10441, London E14 8WR. Cheques payable to London League Publications Ltd. Credit card orders through our website: www.llpshop.co.uk

Books about three great players:

The Great Bev

The rugby league career of Brian Bevan
By Robert Gate

Brian Bevan is one of the few rugby league players to rightfully be called a Legend. He scored 796 tries in British rugby league, a record that will never be surpassed. He had remarkable fitness, pace, side-step and anticipation for try scoring. The book covers his complete rugby league career and memories of him from fellow players and supporters. Lavishly illustrated, the book also has a comprehensive statistical record.
Published in August 2002 at £14.95, post free.
ISBN: 1-903659-06-X

I, George Nepia

The Autobiography of a Rugby Legend
By George Nepia and Terry McLean
Foreword by Oma Nepia - New edition with new material

George Nepia is arguably New Zealand's greatest ever Rugby Union player, Aged 19, he played every game for the 1924-5 'Invincibles' tour of England, Wales, Ireland and France. First published in 1963, this edition has new material that gives a full picture of Nepia's life and rugby career, including a new chapter by his original collaborator, Terry McLean. Also includes a full record of his time in Rugby League.
Published in September 2002 at £13.95.   ISBN: 1903659-07-8.
Special offer for readers of this book: £5.00 post free.

Kiwis, Wigan and The Wire

My Life and Rugby League
By Ces Mountford

Ces Mountford is recognised as one of the greatest Kiwi Rugby League players of all time. He joined Wigan in 1946, and was a key member of the great post-war Wigan team. In 1951, he was the first foreign player to win the Lance Todd Trophy. In 1951, he joined Warrington as manager and stayed for 10 years. He then returned to New Zealand, and developed Rugby League coaching, including managing the national team.
Published in May 2003 at £9.95, post free. ISBN: 1903659-10-8

All 3 books for £25. Order from: London League Publications, PO Box 10441, London E14 8WR. Cheques to London League Publications Ltd.

More Rugby League books

133

Cougars Going Up!
Keighley Cougars Rugby League 2003 Yearbook
Edited by David Kirkley
Records of a great season and lots of club history as well.
Published March 2004, ISBN: 1903659-15-9. £7.95 post free.

Kevin Sinfield Life with Leeds Rhinos
A 2003 Rugby League Diary
By Kevin Sinfield with Philip Gordos
The inside story of Leeds's dramatic season.
Published November 2003, ISBN: 1903659-13-2. £9.95 post free.

A Westminster XIII
Parliamentarians and Rugby League
Edited by David Hinchliffe MP
Contributions from Frank Dobson MP, Lord Geoffrey Lofthouse, Sir Brian Mawhinney MP, Ian NcCartney MP and many more on their favourite sport.
Published November 2002. ISBN: 1903659-08-6 at £9.95.
Special offer: £8.00.

Rugby League Bravehearts
The History of Scottish Rugby League
By Gavin Willacy
The full story of the national team, interviews and profiles of Scottish players, students and development.
Published June 2002. ISBN: 1903659-05-1 at £9.95.
Special offer: £5.00.

Tries in the Valleys
A History of Rugby League in Wales
Edited by Peter Lush and Dave Farrar
Published in April 1998 at £14.95. ISBN: 0952606437.
Special offer: £5.00

Order from London League Publications Ltd, PO Box 10441, London E14 8WR. Cheques to London League Publications Ltd.

Rugby League Analysis, History & Vision

Published twice a year at £2.50

The magazine for Rugby League supporters who want an in-depth analysis of the game.

Four issue subscription: £9.00 (cover price £2.50).
Back numbers available: 1 to 8: £1.50 each or £8 for all 7.
Special £12 offer:
Three issue subscription plus a copy of **one** of the following books:

* *Tries in the Valleys – A History of Rugby League in Wales*
* *From Fulham to Wembley – 20 years of Rugby League in London*
* *The Fulham Dream – Rugby League comes to London*
* *Rugby League Bravehearts – A history of Scottish Rugby League*

SUBSCRIPTION FORM

I would like the following subscription: (tick box)
4 issues - £9.00   []
3 issues plus a book £12.00   []

Subscription to start with issue no.:
Book chosen (3 issue sub):
Back numbers at £1.50 each:
Full set of back numbers - £8:   []

Name:

Address:

Telephone: Email:

Please send to: London League Publications Ltd, Po Box 10441, London E14 0SB. Cheques payable to London League Publications Ltd. Credit card orders via our website: www.llpshop.co.uk. **Photocopy** if you do not want to cut the book, or provide these details when you order.

135